REAL ANSWERS

The TRUE STORY told by GARY CORNWELL,
Deputy Chief Counsel for the U.S. House of Representatives Select
Committee on Assassinations, in charge of the investigation of the
JOHN F. KENNEDY ASSASSINATION

Paleface Press
Spicewood, Texas

Acknowledgments

My love and appreciation to my wife and family and many thanks to my friends who read the drafts, served as my editors and proof readers, and provided suggestions and encouragement. Particularly, I thank my friends for keeping their promises—which, I admit, I coerced them into making—to sugarcoat their suggestions for improvements to the earlier drafts; and Kent Hanson, who plowed through successive drafts, and for so long has been such a great friend that he didn't need to sugarcoat his criticisms. Finally, it goes without saying, but I want to say anyway, that I will always be indebted to my friend Bob Blakey for offering me the job as Deputy Chief Counsel for the Select Committee on Assassinations, and to my father who kept me from refusing the offer—it turned out to be an experience that altered my view of the world.

Contents

Author's Note

It was April 1979, when I completed my work as Deputy Chief Counsel for the Select Committee on Assassinations and we sent the Committee's final report on the assassination of President John F. Kennedy to the Government Printing Office. Over the years since then, I have been asked questions about the case by almost everyone I have met. I have always been amazed at the intense interest and the extensive knowledge that people have of the basic facts, the central issues, and the principal "conspiracy theories." At the same time I have been surprised by the lack of public knowledge of the findings of the Select Committee. (So, you worked on the Warren Commission? Oh! What was the Select Committee on Assassinations?)

Public knowledge of the case has been confined almost entirely to secondary sources of information — newspaper articles, books by private citizens setting forth conspiracy theories, motion pictures and television shows. Although some of that information has been admittedly fictionalized, most of it has purported to be "documentary." Yet real, honest answers to the eternal issues in the case have seldom been given, in large part because the results of the extensive investigation by the Select Committee on Assassinations have been unknown, or in some cases, to satisfy other agendas, have been purposely ignored.

Some years ago, while I was living in Denver, a public furor arose over the "two-Oswald theory." The newspapers reported "new" speculation that Lee Harvey Oswald, the man whom the Warren Commission in 1964 announced was the sole person responsible for the assassination, was really two different people, one who defected to Russia in 1959, and another (imposter) who returned from Russia in 1962 to kill the president. This time, the furor was over whether or not the body of the Oswald who had been killed by Jack Ruby less than 48 hours after the assassination of the president, should be removed from its grave and reinspected (for height, dental, and other unique identifying characteristics). For weeks the newspapers were full of stories debating the pros and cons of whether to exhume the body. During this time, my friends frequently asked me, "What do you think they will find if they dig up the body?" I told them that this was not a new conspiracy theory, and that the Select Committee on Assassinations had conducted an extensive investigation of the issue. Our handwriting identification experts compared letters written by Oswald before, during and after his trip to Russia. Our photographic experts and our forensic anthropologists examined pictures taken of him before, during and after Russia. We learned from both photographic and medical experts that apparent height differences, as measured in police lineup photos and as measured while he lay on the autopsy table after he was killed, were not significant or suspicious, and did not in fact support the theory of two Oswalds. Our experts explained that the *apparent* height of a suspect as reflected in a police lineup photo is determined by the height (and thus view angle) of the camera; and that because of the compression of the spine when standing, people are shorter when standing than when lying down in a prone position (such as, on an autopsy table). I told my friends that my belief, based upon our investigation, was that the two-Oswald theory is contrary to the available scientific evidence, and that if they exhumed the body they would find the one and only Lee Harvey Oswald.

What was most interesting to me was that not once in any of the newspaper articles that I saw was the investigation of the Select Committee on Assassinations ever mentioned. The articles only rehashed the historical rationales for believing in the possibility of two Oswalds. There was no mention that the Select Committee on Assassinations extensively investigated these rationales; no mention of all of the scientific evidence on the subject that was set forth in its final report; no mention even that the committee ever existed. From the newspaper accounts, it appeared as if this was some new theory, based upon newly discovered evidence, that needed to be look into. Well, the body was finally exhumed, and the new inspection confirmed that it was the body of the one and only Lee Harvey Oswald.

My point is not that the investigation of the Select Committee answered all questions relating to the Kennedy case. Nor do I suggest that the American public should necessarily accept the findings of the Select Committee as the last word on any question related to the Kennedy case. My point is that I know from twenty years of talking to people about the subject that what the Select Committee did is of great interest to the American public, and that if the news media felt that the possibility of digging up Oswald's body was of interest to the public, then the result of the Select Committee's scientific investigation of the issue was relevant information to report—to say nothing of simply being interesting.

That most people have derived their information about the case from secondary sources is also indicated by my own (admittedly not-very-scientific) survey over the past several months. I created a Web site on the Internet to announce the writing of this book, and to solicit comments and questions that would help me in writing the book. I asked that each person who submitted a comment also tell me how many books they had read on the subject, and among those books, whether they had read the Warren Commission Report or the Report of the Select Committee on Assassinations. About 1/3 of those who provided comments indicated that they had not read any previous book on the subject. Of the 2/3 who had read a book or books on the subject (including many who had read dozens), over 1/3 of those had not read the Warren Commission's report, and only a few had read the Select Committee's final report. These figures are probably explained in large part by the fact that while it is sometimes possible to find a copy of the Warren Commission Report in a bookstore, no publisher (apparently) has published the final Report of the Select Committee on Assassinations since its only non-governmental publication by Bantam Books in July 1979.

Notwithstanding the heavy reliance upon often unreliable secondary sources of information, almost everyone I have talked to over the years has had a very definite opinion about the case. In particular, everyone either believes there was, or there was not, a conspiracy—few people seem to have no opinion—and everyone seems to have many (sometimes, unalterable) reasons to support their position. Occasionally, I have even found it difficult to get a word in myself, as their enthusiasm for their views spills forth. (The case certainly does capture our imaginations!)

I do not, however, fault those who may hold "uninformed" opinions. As a trial lawyer, I have learned that the human mind cannot focus on a vacuum, so it creates an image (if none is provided) to give content to thought. Thus, if I were to tell you that I live on a lake near Austin, Texas, a picture of the house would quite naturally form in your mind. If I didn't take the time or care enough to actually describe the house to you, your image of the house probably would not be very accurate, but it would be just as real to you as if

I had actually described it to you or shown you a photo of it. Similarly, you may have had the experience of "meeting" someone for the first time over the telephone, and then being quite surprised when you finally met them in person to find that they didn't look anything like you had pictured them in your mind.

Recent studies reflect that 78% of the American public believes there was a conspiracy, which means that 78% of the American public does not believe our government's conclusion when the case was first investigated in 1963–64. That vacuum has had exactly the same effect as if no answer had ever been provided—people have done the best thing they could under the circumstances, namely, create their own answers and their own reasons to support them.

If there is some criticism to be leveled in this regard, it should be leveled as much at me as at anyone else. (Let he who is without blame cast the first stone.) I ran the investigation for the U.S. House of Representatives Select Committee on Assassinations, and yet I have never before made any real effort to make available to the American public what I learned from running that investigation. Begging your pardon for the delay, I offer this book in the spirit of "better late than never."

The questions and answers are not set out in order of importance. Nor are answers to the most commonly asked questions at the front. So, you may want to simply skip to the questions that are of most interest to you.

On the other hand, the main reason to study the Kennedy case—particularly, now, so many years after the event—is probably to discover the lessons it holds about life. Thus, the greatest value probably comes not from reading someone else's conclusion about "what happened," but from the process of personally thinking through the questions of *how* and *why* it happened. In addition, I suspect that some of you may want to evaluate not only the information I provide, but also its source, in the case. If those concepts appeal to you, you may want to start reading from the beginning.

What happened on November 22, 1963?
(Just the Facts.)

John F. Kennedy, the 35th President of the United States, was shot to death on November 22, 1963, while riding in a motorcade in Dallas, Texas.

That was the first sentence from the first chapter of the final Report of the Select Committee on Assassinations. In a very real sense, those are the only facts that have been without significant dispute in the thirty-five years since the tragic event. As you will learn by reading this book, if you are not already aware, that tragic event was followed by a tragic investigation, which in turn was followed by thirty-five years of often misguided and sometimes reckless speculation and misinformation about the available evidence.

Kennedy became the youngest ever president of the

United States in 1960 by narrowly defeating his Republican opponent, Vice President Richard Nixon, by 118,450 votes out of nearly 69 million votes cast. Despite the slim election victory, Kennedy's initial popularity was great. His youth, good looks, wealth, intelligence and determination gave him a unique magic and power that made people feel strongly about him, both those who loved and admired him, and those who hated and feared him.

The early 1960's were times filled with high stakes and volatile political, social and economic changes, both at home and abroad; times characterized by passion, intractable positions, and violence. As the fall of 1963 approached, Kennedy's popularity had declined to 59 percent from its high of 83 percent in the spring of 1961, and his concern for the upcoming 1964 election led him to schedule a trip to Texas, the home state of his Vice-President, Lyndon Johnson, where he hoped to shore up his falling popularity by touring the major cities of Houston, San Antonio, Ft. Worth and Dallas.

Kennedy enjoyed traveling, and was essentially reckless in ignoring the protective measures that the Secret Service urged him to adopt. Only once (during another trip in November, 1963, to Chicago) did he allow his limousine to be flanked by police officers on motorcycles, and he never allowed Secret Service officers to ride on the rear bumper of the limousine. He was philosophical about the danger, believing that assassination was a risk inherent in a democratic society. In fact, during the November trip to Dallas, President Kennedy told a White House assistant that if anybody really wanted to shoot him, it would not be a very difficult job, since "all they would have to do is get on a high building with a telescopic rifle, and there is nothing anybody could do to defend against such an attempt."

Kennedy had lost considerable public support in the South, mainly because of his active civil rights program. Newsweek magazine, in fact, reported in October 1963, that no Democratic president had ever been so disliked in the South. Of the major Texas cities, Dallas was particularly troubling. As summarized in the final Report of the Select Committee on Assassinations, Dallas was viewed as:

> . . . a violent, hysterical center of right-wing fanaticism. There, in 1960, then-Texas Senator Lyndon B. Johnson had been heckled and spat upon. In October 1963, just a month before the President's scheduled visit, Ambassador to the United Nations Adlai Stevenson was jeered, hit with a placard and spat upon. Byron Skelton, the National Democratic Committeeman from Texas, wrote Attorney General Robert Kennedy about his concern for President Kennedy's safety and urged him to dissuade his brother from going to Texas.

The Dallas newspapers announced on September 13 that Kennedy was coming to Texas; the Governor of Texas, John Connally, announced the itinerary for the president's trip through Texas on November 1; the final motorcade route for the Dallas visit was selected on November 15 and (at the urging of Kennedy's staff) the route was published in the Dallas newspapers on November 18 and 19. Lee Harvey

Oswald had returned from Mexico to Dallas in early October, and secured a position at the School Book Depository on October 15.

Although the Secret Service had received 34 threats on the president's life from Texas during the preceding two years, and had generally identified six categories of persons who posed a potential threat (right-wing extremists, left-wing extremists, Cubans, Puerto Ricans, Black militants, and miscellaneous mental cases), political embarrassment was the chief concern for the Dallas trip. During the week prior to the trip, defamatory posters and leaflets were widely distributed in Dallas, and on the Friday morning of the motorcade, a full-page advertisement sponsored by the "America-thinking Citizens of Dallas" appeared in the Dallas Morning News, charging that Kennedy had ignored the Constitution, scrapped the Monroe Doctrine in favor of the "Spirit of Moscow," and become "soft on Communists, fellow-travelers, and ultra-leftists in America."

President Kennedy and his wife arrived in Texas on Thursday, November 21. They first visited Houston and San Antonio, where they were greeted by enthusiastic crowds, and then flew to Ft. Worth to spend the night. On Friday morning it was raining in Ft. Worth when Kennedy addressed the Chamber of Commerce, a speech that Governor Connally later described as being laced with fun, and very well received. Kennedy told his staff that if the weather cleared, he did not want to use the protective bubble on the limousine during the motorcade in Dallas. As Air Force One took off for Dallas, Kennedy remarked to Governor Connally that it looked like they in were in luck and were going to get sunshine.

When they arrived in Dallas it was a gorgeous fall day, 68 degrees with clear blue skies. They were met by an enthusiastic crowd of about 400. After shaking hands and greeting those at the edges of the crowd, President Kennedy and his wife Jackie joined Governor Connally and his wife Nellie in the presidential limousine. The president sat in the rear seat on the right, with Governor Connally in a jump seat in front of him. Their wives sat on their left. Two secret service agents occupied the front seat.

The motorcade was led by two cars containing Dallas Police Chief Jesse Curry and other members of the police force and Secret Service. The presidential limousine was third, followed by a car with White House staff and Secret Service agents (who stood on the running boards), then a limousine with Vice President Lyndon Johnson and his wife and Texas Senator Ralph Yarborough, and finally a long line of follow-up cars carrying members of Congress, other dignitaries, photographers, members of the White House staff and others.

As the motorcade left the Love Field airport at about 11:50 a.m., Governor Connally remained worried that some political embarrassment or demonstration would occur, or that the crowds would be unfriendly, indifferent or sullen, and mar the president's trip to Texas that, up until then, had been so positive.

But as the motorcade neared the center of the city, Governor Connally's fears began to subside:

> The further we got toward town, the denser became the crowds, and when we got down on Main Street, the crowds were extremely thick. They were pushed off of curbs; they were out in the street, and they were backed all the way up against the walls of the buildings. They were just as thick as they could be. I don't know how many. But, there were at least a quarter of a million people on the parade route that day and everywhere the reception was good.

The Governor noticed that Mrs. Kennedy seemed to become more relaxed and was enjoying the crowds. When a lone heckler held up a placard reading, "Kennedy Go Home," the president light heartedly said, "Don't you imagine he's a nice fellow," and the Governor replied, "Yes, I imagine he's a nice fellow." Apart from that incident, Connally described the reception as being "more enthusiastic than I could have hoped for." A little girl held up a sign containing the request, "President Kennedy, will you shake hands with me?" The president had the limousine stop, he shook hands with the little girl, and the car was mobbed by admirers who had to be separated from the president by the Secret Service agents. Closer to downtown, the president again had the limousine stop so he could talk to a Catholic nun and her group of school children. Again, enthusiastic supporters rushed from the curb to greet the president, and had to be restrained by Secret Service agents.

As the motorcade neared Dealey Plaza, the crowds grew larger, packing the sidewalks, hanging out of office building windows, and cheering, and it was clear that President Kennedy was delighted with his Dallas reception. In Governor Connally's words, ". . . the trip had been absolutely wonderful, and we were heaving a sigh of relief because once we got through the motorcade at Dallas and through the Dallas luncheon, then everything else was pretty much routine."

After the limousine turned into Dealey Plaza and headed north on Houston Street toward the Texas School Book Depository one block ahead, Mrs. Connally turned to the president and said, "Mr. President, you can't say Dallas doesn't love you." "That's obvious," he said in response.

The limousine made a hairpin turn in front of the Book Depository, and headed west on Elm Street. It was about 12:30 p.m.; the president was waving to the crowds as shots rang out.

Mrs. Connally turned to her right and saw the president put both hands over his neck, then slump down into the seat. Thinking the noise was a rifle shot, the Governor first turned to his right, attempting to see the president. He later said:

> . . . I never made the full turn. About the time I turned back where I was facing more or less straight ahead, the way the car was moving, I was hit. I was knocked over, just doubled over by the force of the bullet. It went in my back and came out my chest about 2 inches below and to the left of my right

nipple. The force of the bullet drove my body over almost double, and when I looked, immediately I could see I was drenched with blood. So, I knew I had been badly hit and I more or less straightened up. At about this time, Nellie reached over and pulled me down into her lap.

I was in her lap facing forward when another shot was fired . . . I did not hear the shot that hit me. I wasn't conscious of it. I am sure I heard it, but I was not conscious of it at all. I heard another shot. I heard it hit. It hit with a very pronounced impact . . . it made a very, very strong sound.

Immediately, I could see blood and brain tissue all over the interior of the car and all over our clothes. We were both covered with brain tissue, and there were pieces of brain tissue as big as your little finger.

※   ※   ※

When I was hit, or shortly before I was hit—no, I guess it was after I was hit—I said first, just almost in despair, I said, "no, no, no," just thinking how tragic it was that we had gone through this 24 hours, it had all been so wonderful and so beautifully executed.

The President had been so marvelously received and then here, at the last moment, this great tragedy. I just said, "no, no, no, no." Then I said right after I was hit, I said, "My God, they are going to kill us all."

Initially thinking that her husband was dead as he lay in her lap, Mrs. Connally did not look back, but after one of the shots, she heard Mrs. Kennedy say, "They have shot my husband." Then, after another shot, she heard Mrs. Kennedy say, "They have killed my husband. I have his brains in my hand."

The limousine accelerated and sped toward Parkland Hospital. According to Mrs. Connally, "There was no screaming in that horrible car. It was just a silent, terrible drive." At 1:00 p.m., President Kennedy was pronounced dead.

So, exactly what was the
Select Committee on Assassinations?
(And how did you get involved?)

On November 29, 1963, seven days after the assassination, President Lyndon Johnson signed Executive Order No. 11130 creating the Warren Commission. The Warren Commission was a "blue-ribbon" panel headed by U.S. Supreme Court Justice Earl Warren. Its charge—at least its "official" charge—was to evaluate "all the facts and circumstances surrounding the assassination and the subsequent killing of the alleged assassin Lee Harvey Oswald," and to report its findings and conclusions to President Johnson, and the American public.

Ten months later, on September 24, 1964, the Warren Commission delivered its report, announcing that President Kennedy had been killed by Lee Harvey Oswald, acting alone, and that there was no conspiracy. The Warren Commission Report was met with immediate public skepticism. Over the following years, as the proceedings and conclusions of the Warren Commission were studied, more and more disparities and apparent contradictions between the "evidence" and the "findings" were uncovered that had no readily apparent explanations. The mounting questions led to rejection of the Warren Commission's findings, and ultimately to suspicions that there had been an intentional coverup of the facts, perhaps because the federal government itself was involved in the assassination. Over the following fourteen years, literally hundreds of books and thousands of news articles piled up, offering a smorgasbord of conspiracy theories to fill the credibility void left by the Warren Commission's report.

The widespread public rejection of the conclusions of the Warren Commission finally led Congress to fund a second investigation. To conduct the new inquiry, Congress created the Select Committee on Assassinations, a special committee of the U.S. House of Representatives. The main offices of the Committee were located in Washington, D.C.

Because it was not part of the Executive Branch, the Select Committee had no right to charge anyone with a crime, and because it was not part of the Judicial Branch of government, it had no right to determine anyone's guilt or innocence in a court of law. As a congressional committee, the Select Committee did have investigative powers, but only as an incident to its prime function, which was to recommend new legislation if the Committee determined through investigation that changes in our laws should be made. But in spite of its official function of recommending legislation, everyone recognized that the real purpose of the Committee was to investigate and attempt to answer the question, "Who was responsible for the murder of President John F. Kennedy?"

When I took over as Deputy Chief Counsel for the Committee on September 1, 1977, a staff of approximately 45 attorneys, investigators and researchers was already assembled. My job was to determine how to make the most effective use of those resources. First thing in the morning on the first day of my new job, everyone gathered in one of the congressional offices for introductions. As I took a seat at the head of the long conference table, looking at the 45 new faces, I said, "I'll bet the main question on all of your minds is, how did I get this job?" Everyone laughed, indicating that I was correct. So I proceeded, "I got the job the same way everyone in Washington gets jobs—I knew someone."

The person I knew was G. Robert Blakey. Earlier that summer, Blakey had been appointed as the Committee's Chief Counsel. In that capacity, he was in charge of the overall work of the Committee, which involved both the Kennedy investigation, and the investigation of the death of Martin Luther King. Blakey recommended me to head the Kennedy investigation, and another lawyer to head the King investigation (although soon thereafter, the Deputy Chief Counsel for the King investigation left the committee, and Blakey ran the King investigation himself).

I knew Blakey from my years with the Organized Crime Section of the Justice Department. I joined the Justice Department in 1970 upon graduation from law school, and began work in Washington, D.C. One of my first assignments was to write a law review article for Wil Wilson, the Assistant Attorney General for the Criminal Division. In the article, I reviewed the provisions of the 1970 Organized Crime Control Act, which was in the final stages of becoming law. Bob Blakey (whom I did not know at the time) had been the principal architect of this legislation, which he drafted in the U.S. Senate as Chief Counsel for Senator McClellan's Judiciary Committee.

Some months later, in the fall of 1970, I was transferred from Washington to Kansas City in connection with the new Organized Crime Strike Force that was to open there. I was the first lawyer on the scene, and immediately took over the prosecution of a pending case against Nick Civella, the head of the Mafia in Kansas City. Just before I arrived in Kansas City, a low level Mafia associate had hired four black men to "silence" one of the two principal witnesses in the case, a scrap metal dealer named Sol Landie, which they accomplished by shooting him in the head while he lay in bed next to his wife. The other remaining principal witness was another scrap metal dealer named Alvin Hurst.

The life of Mr. Hurst—as well as the prospect of successfully convicting Nicholas Civella—was obviously in jeopardy. Historically, in federal criminal cases, there had been no pretrial procedure to preserve the testimony of a wit-

13

ness for use as evidence at trial. However, the Preservation of Testimony Statute which Blakey drafted as part of the 1970 Organized Crime Control Act, had just become law on October 15, 1970.

This provided the occasion for my first conversation with Blakey. This was to be the first time that the new statute would be used in the country, and I needed to provide the judge with some suggestions about how to handle the new procedure. Because no one in the Justice Department knew as much about the statute as Blakey did, I called Blakey for guidance. Thanks to Blakey and his statute, I was able to save what was left of the case against Nick Civella by preserving the testimony of the other principal witness—and in the process, protect his life by removing some of the incentive to silence him.

I remained in Kansas City for seven years, ultimately becoming Chief of the Strike Force. During those years, as I investigated and tried organized crime cases for the Kansas City Strike Force, I frequently needed to use the other statutes that also became law as part of the 1970 Act. I would often call Blakey and ask him how he thought the various statutes should work, what the "legislative intent" was and how it could be used in addressing legal issues about the statutes' proper interpretation and meaning, and what arguments or legal precedents he would suggest I use in responding to challenges about the statutes' constitutionality. In one of those cases, one of the first in the country involving the Special Danger Offender Sentencing Statute that was part of the 1970 Act, Blakey filed an *amicus curiae* brief as a supplement to the appellate brief that I wrote for the government in the U.S. Court of Appeals for the Eighth Circuit. It was through these events that I got to know Blakey.

In June of 1977, after conducting the sentencing hearing and thus finally concluding the case against Nick Civella which I had started in 1970, Civella was sent off to prison and I left the Justice Department. Since I had taken no vacation during my seven years with the Organized Crime Section, my plan was to take some time off, travel to Alaska (a life-long desire), and then move to Colorado to practice law. Although I didn't know it at the time, that same month Blakey was appointed Chief Counsel for the Select Committee on Assassinations.

I stopped in Houston for a couple of weeks to visit my parents and play golf with my father before leaving for Alaska. Blakey somehow found me there. He called to tell me about his plans for the Select Committee's investigation of the Kennedy case, and asked me to come to Washington and run the investigation for the Select Committee. He said that he wanted to fly me to Washington, show me the committee offices, and talk about what we could accomplish. I told him that I really wasn't interested. I had been to Washington and really didn't like the politics, and even though I very much enjoyed hunting and fishing in the forests and streams of the beautiful Virginia countryside, the east coast always made me feel fenced in. (I am obviously a wide-open-spaces western spirit at heart.) I told Blakey I was just

15

leaving on a trip to Alaska, and then planned to move to Colorado. Blakey asked me to think about it, and call him back. I agreed.

I walked outside and told my father about the phone call, stating that I was not inclined to take the job. My father said that was one of the dumbest things he had ever heard me say, that this was a once in a lifetime opportunity that any lawyer would (or should!) love to have, and that I would be a fool if I didn't change my mind.

A few days later, I took off in my father's mobile home, together with my wife and a couple of friends, headed for Alaska. Along the way I kept thinking about Blakey's offer, and my father's pointed advice. Finally, I stopped at a pay phone booth in Colorado and called Blakey. I agreed to take him up on his offer to fly to Washington for further discussions. I left my wife and friends in the mobile home, and I flew to Washington.

What most concerned me was the politics. I had been a prosecutor, and even the politics in the Justice Department were hard for me to take. I wasn't anxious to have to put up with even more of the same in the context of a congressional committee. What finally convinced me to take the job was Blakey's promise. He assured me he would handle the task of dealing with the congressional committee members, that I would be free to conduct the investigation, and that I would get all of the support I needed to conduct an effective investigation. I knew there were not very many people in the country who could credibly make such a promise, but I also knew that Blakey could. I said I would take the job.

Blakey agreed that I could complete an abbreviated version of the vacation trip I was in the middle of, so I flew back to Colorado, drove the mobile home through California and back to Texas, then flew to Washington and started work on September 1, 1977. (I still have not yet made it to Alaska.)

What about all of the Mysterious Deaths?
What about the Umbrella Man, and the
Three Tramps?
What about the fake photos of Oswald
holding a Mannlicher-Carcano rifle
and Communist newspaper?

The Mysterious Deaths, the Umbrella Man, and the Three Tramps, together with photos of other mystery men who were photographed in and around Dealey Plaza on November 22, 1963, and who purportedly included Watergate conspirators, CIA agents and right-wing extremists—these were simply a few of the hundreds of conspiracy theories that had captured the public's imagination as a result of the books and articles that were written between 1963 and 1977. In addition, there were allegations of faked photos, of planted

18

evidence, of destroyed evidence, and innumerable other challenges to the Warren Commission's conclusion that Oswald fired the bullets that killed the president. Deciding where to start was a daunting task, to say the least.

We began by reviewing all of the available literature that had been written on the subject of the Kennedy case. From that literature, we listed the issues and conspiracy theories that had been raised, and then on huge charts organized the issues and theories into categories by subject matter. Next, we tried to decide which specific issues and allegations could still be investigated effectively 15 years after the crime was committed; and for those that could, whether what we learned was likely to shed significant new light on the two big questions in the case—who fired the fatal bullets, and whether there was a conspiracy.

Finally, we broke the overall conspiracy issue into separate parts so we could focus upon each of the major groups of "suspects" who had the motive, opportunity and means to kill the president, in essence simply assuming that "where there is smoke, there may be fire." Thus, one of the major areas of investigation that we focused upon was a possible Mafia conspiracy, both because the Kennedy administration's crackdown on organized crime, headed by the president's brother, Attorney General Robert Kennedy, clearly gave the Mafia a motive that made them suspects in the case, and because it appeared that at least Jack Ruby, if not Oswald, had Mafia connections.

We then split the staff into teams, with each team of

attorneys, researchers and investigators being assigned to investigate one or more of the major issues. There was a Mafia team, a Castro (Cuban) team, an anti-Castro team, a government-conspiracy team, etc. The official "legislative" function of determining whether new laws should be enacted certainly did not consume our attention or constitute the daily focus of our work. We wanted to solve the case.

For the first several months, as we progressed through the list of issues, most of our investigation actually resulted in discrediting the numerous conspiracy theories that had grown up over the years. But we hoped that if we looked in enough places, if we had some luck, and *if there really was* a conspiracy, we would find evidence of it.

I can still remember where I was when I heard the news!

The passage of time between the occurrence of a crime and the evidence gathering process is always a detriment in a criminal investigation. The phrase most often used to describe the problem is "a cold trail," which I assume is a phrase that must have originated with some Tombstone sheriff in the Old West who was bemoaning the problem of trying to follow the trail of some bad guy across the prairie, days or weeks after the hoof prints were largely obliterated by wind and rain. In modern day criminal investigations, the evidence from which the bad guys are typically caught is not broken twigs or distinctive hoof marks in the mud, but a fresh trail is just as important as it used to be. In modern criminal investigations, the stuff from which cases are solved, if they are going to be solved, typically consists of important words that someone spoke, a reconstruction of the precise timing of events, the scientific analysis of splattered blood or other fragile physical evidence that is often perishable and/or subject to adulteration, and a myriad of other evidentiary details that are seldom carved in stone for future generations to inspect. In a case of major public concern such as the Kennedy case, the lapse of time also geometrically increases the difficulty in judging witness credibility, not only in evaluating why a witness did not provide information sooner, but also in trying to assess the influence of intervening news media commentary and public speculations upon a witness's desire and ability to provide accurate testimony.

To put the problem into perspective with the Kennedy case, if you were a teenager or older when Kennedy was killed, you could still remember in 1978 (15 years later) where you were when you heard the news of his death. Most people—even some who were only five years old in 1963— tell me they can still clearly remember, even today. So, if an investigator in 1978 were to ask you where you were when Kennedy was killed, you could—if you desired to do so— provide that fact to assist in the investigation. But if you were asked questions about who you knew on November 22, 1963, you probably could not remember whether you met certain people before or after November, 1963. Similarly, you probably could not remember where you were on the evening of November 21, or what you did during the week before November 22. It is such details upon which most criminal investigations depend for the solution to murder cases, and which in large part had already been lost before the Select Committee on Assassinations started its investigation in 1977.

But all was not lost by the passage of time. First, a lot of the important physical evidence had been gathered in the original investigation, and was still available, including the Mannlicher-Carcano rifle taken from the School Book Depository, the lead fragments taken from the limousine, detailed photographs taken during the course of the autopsy, and many photographs taken in Dealey Plaza as the motorcade passed by and shots were fired. We even found significant new physical evidence that had never been discovered during the course of the Warren Commission. Tape recordings made by the Dallas Police Department that contained sounds apparently transmitted from a motorcycle in the motorcade at the time of the shooting were a prominent example of "newly discovered" physical evidence that the Select Committee found, even after fifteen years.

To learn as much as possible from the great quantity of available physical evidence, we devoted a large part of our investigative resources to science, specifically, to the scientific analysis of that physical evidence. We hired nationally renowned handwriting experts to analyze Oswald's writings (or, more specifically, to determine if all of the writings were from "the same Oswald"). We had forensic anthropologists provide expert opinions on morphological features and bone structures in order to identify persons in questioned photographs, including both Oswald and others whom many believed were conspirators (e.g., the "three tramps"). We conducted neutron activation analysis on the bullet fragments found in the limousine. To a large extent, we were able to re-conduct the autopsy by using 3-D viewing techniques made possible by the large number of photos that had been taken during the course of the original autopsy, and thereby correct significant errors that had been made in the original 1963 autopsy by clinical pathologists who lacked the proper training in forensic pathology methodology. We put together perhaps the greatest panel of photographic experts ever assembled, to analyze the photographic evidence, investigate allegations of forged or altered photographs (e.g., the Oswald "back yard" photos), and construct clear photos of suspects where none had been available before.

Our photographic panel, through a sophisticated analysis of the shadows in the "mysterious" Oswald back-yard photos (which many people, including Oswald, had alleged were composite fakes), was able to determine the precise position of the sun and thus the time of year when the photos were taken. Our photo experts extracted emulsion dots from photos, ran them through computers, and created the first clear photos of many of the suspects in the case (a technique that we take for granted today, but was cutting edge science in 1977). NASA experts performed a trajectory analysis to better determine where the shots came from that hit the president, using more accurate data about the location of bullet wounds developed by our forensic pathologists, and improved information about the positions of the occupants in the presidential limousine developed by our photo experts. Neutron activation analysis—a technique that involved bombarding the various lead fragments found in the limousine with neutrons to determine how many different *bullets* the fragments may have come from—allowed us to determine how many different bullets probably hit the limousine. And the nation's leading experts on acoustics analyzed the tape recordings that we discovered had been made by the Dallas Police Department when a stuck microphone on a motorcycle apparently transmitted the sounds of gun fire from Dealey Plaza, to determine whether the recordings contained evidence of more than one shooter.

The other major area in which we invested our investigative resources was in the review of historical files that no one had previously bothered to read with a view to unraveling the Kennedy assassination. The object, of course, was to overcome the loss of memory that had occurred over the intervening fifteen years, by reviewing available government files that had been created in the early 1960's, and contained records of relevant events, recorded when they were fresh in people's minds.

In pursuit of this objective, we negotiated "unsanitized" access to the CIA's files—something that had never before been granted to a congressional committee. Under the agreed procedure, the backgrounds of all of our staff members were investigated, and after receiving "top secret" security clearances, we were allowed to review relevant CIA files without any redaction (deletion) of the CIA's "sources and methods." We then wrote reports summarizing the facts reflected in the classified files. The CIA then had the right to review the final summary reports before they were published. Although the phraseology in the final public reports that were published at the conclusion of our investigation was subject to negotiation in order to prevent the disclosure of sensitive sources and methods, we remained free to disclose our conclusions, in other words, the "facts" as we saw them. We made extensive use of CIA files in our investigation of possible pro-Castro and anti-Castro conspiracy issues (including activities in and around New Orleans at the time that Oswald was there in the summer of 1963; and Oswald's mysterious alleged visit to anti-Castro activist Sylvia Odio and his trip to Mexico City in September 1963); in investigating the issue of a possible Russian conspiracy suggested by the defection in January, 1964 of a high-level KGB officer named Yuri Nosenko (who coincidentally said he had reviewed the KGB file on Oswald); and in investigating the can-of-worms CIA/Mafia/Cuban assassination plots.

Illuminating new insights into the case—insights, incidentally, that stood in stark contrast to the Warren Commission's findings—also came from our review of the extensive transcripts of Mafia conversations that the FBI had secured through illegal electronic surveillance in the early 1960's. Most of the major organized crime families (with two prominent exceptions, Carlos Marcello in New Orleans and Santos Trafficante in Florida) were the subject of this eavesdropping, and the transcripts contained numerous conversations where killing Kennedy was proposed, discussed and debated by Mafia leaders.

We even managed to develop some significant new information through traditional interviews of witnesses, in spite of the fact that the vast majority of such evidence had been lost as a result of the intervening years. One of the best examples of a newly discovered witness was Jack Ray Tatum, a previously unknown eye witness to the killing of Dallas Police Officer Tippit. The Warren Commission concluded that Tippit was shot by Lee Harvey Oswald in a residential neighborhood in the Oak Cliff area of Dallas, less than 1 mile from Oswald's rooming house, approximately 45 minutes after the assassination of the president. The previously known facts were that Officer Tippit (for reasons that have been the subject of much speculation) was patrolling the neighborhood in his car and (also for reasons that have been questioned) apparently recognized Oswald walking on the sidewalk. Tippit apparently said something to Oswald, got out of his car, and was immediately shot by Oswald. The Select Committee reviewed the historical eyewitness and physical evidence, and agreed with the basic conclusion of the Warren Commission that Oswald killed Tippit.

However, Mr. Tatum, who had never been interviewed by the Warren Commission and was discovered by one of the Select Committee's investigators, provided some disturbing new evidence about the final moments of the Oswald-Tippit encounter, evidence that could reasonably be viewed as corroboration for conspiracy theories suggesting that Tippit and Oswald had some unknown pre-existing relationship. Tatum told us that after Tippit got out of his car, Oswald first shot him from his position on the sidewalk, then walked around the patrol car to where Tippit lay in the street, and stood over him while he shot him at point blank range. This action, which is often encountered in gangland murders and is commonly described as a *coup de grace,* is more indicative of an execution than an act of self-defense or escape.

After hearing Tatum's story, we reviewed the Tippit autopsy report, and discovered that it did indeed reflect one bullet wound slanting upward from front to back—just the kind of wound that would have been produced by a shot from someone standing at Tippit's feet while he lay on the ground. This wound had not been—and really cannot be—explained by the earlier evidence gathered by the Warren Commission. The Select Committee unfortunately did not develop any further information of significance on the issue, and the full implications of Mr. Tatum's evidence may never be known.

Another interesting witness whom we interviewed, and who had not previously been questioned in the Kennedy case, was in Cuba. The interview was interesting for many reasons, but partially, simply because (to use a phrase from the Select Committee's final Report), "When the leader of a great nation is assassinated, those . . . suspected always include his adversaries."

Fidel Castro was a suspect in the case because, undoubtedly, he was Kennedy's "adversary." Castro's successful revolution, ending with his arrival in Havana on January 1, 1959, was initially warmly received in the United States. But relations deteriorated quickly with Castro's mass executions of officials of the former Batista government; his nationalization of American property, beginning with the United States-owned Cuban Telephone Company in March 1959; and the defection to the United States in June of Cuban Air Force Major Pedro Diaz Lanz, who reported communist influence in the armed forces and government of Cuba. By the summer of 1960, Castro had seized more than $700 million in U.S. property, his top lieutenant Ernesto "Che" Guevara had publicly announced that the revolution had turned to communism, and President Eisenhower had authorized the CIA to organize and equip Cuban refugees to overthrow Castro. On January 2, 1961, the United States cut off diplomatic relations with Cuba, and in his State of the Union address on January 30, Kennedy railed against "Communist agents seeking to exploit" Latin America's peaceful revolution of hope, and the "domination [of the Cuban people] by foreign and domestic tyrannies."

It was only three months later, in April 1961, that the military force of anti-Castro Cubans organized and financed by our CIA invaded Cuba at the Bay of Pigs. And in October, 1962, the Cuban missile crisis led us to the brink of war with Russia when the U.S. discovered that Russia was installing offensive missiles with nuclear strike capabilities on Cuban soil.

But, as if all of this were not enough to make Castro a suspect, there was also evidence that Castro was—and may have *known* that he was—more than a mere "adversary" of Kennedy. In 1975, the year before the Select Committee on Assassinations was formed, the Senate Select Committee To Study Government Operations published a report on "Alleged Assassination Plots Involving Foreign Leaders." In that report, the Senate committee revealed that:

> United States Government personnel [in the CIA] plotted to kill [Fidel] Castro from 1960 to 1965. American underworld figures [i.e., the Mafia] and Cubans hostile to Castro were used in these plots, and were provided encouragement and material support by the United States [i.e., the CIA].

In short, the Senate investigation uncovered the fact that from 1960 to 1965 the CIA, together with some anti-Castro Cubans and some members of the Mafia, had worked together to assassinate Castro. One of those plots involved the CIA's contacts with an important Cuban official (code named AMLASH) who was trusted by Castro, but who professed an interest in organizing a coup against Castro. That plot was clearly still ongoing in November, 1963. The other plot, which involved the CIA's use of the Mafia, was initiated in 1960 in a conversation between the CIA's Deputy Director for Plans, Richard Bissell, and its Director of Security, Col. Sheffield Edwards. This second plot was actively ongoing until at least February, 1963, and probably longer. Of course, if Castro had learned of those plots prior to November 22, 1963, he could have concluded that his relationship with Kennedy was not merely "adversarial," but indeed a matter of life-and-death, either his or Kennedy's.

It is interesting (and unfortunate) that the CIA never informed the Warren Commission of the assassination plots at a time when the evidentiary details were not so stale, and investigation would have been easier. The Warren Commission did look into other events indicating a possible Cuban conspiracy, including Oswald's distribution of pro-Castro literature for the Fair Play for Cuba Committee in New Orleans in the summer of 1963, and Oswald's trip to Mexico City in September, 1963, where he visited the Soviet Embassy, and the Cuban Embassy and Consulate and attempted to secure a visa to travel to Cuba.

The CIA also provided to the Select Committee evidence from a "highly confidential, but reliable source" that, while Oswald was in the Cuban Consulate, he vowed in the presence of consulate officials to assassinate the president. Coincidentally, an article in the National Enquirer in 1967 by a British freelance writer named Comer Clark, reported that in an exclusive interview Castro stated to Clark that he had heard of such threats by Oswald in the Cuban consulate. Given the source, including the reputation of Clark (author of articles such as "British Girls as Nazi Sex Slaves"), the National Enquirer article easily could have been rejected as a fabrication except for the "highly confidential" corroborating information provided by the CIA, reflecting that the alleged threats were actually made.

In addition, the CIA provided to the Committee a blind memorandum apparently prepared in 1963. The memo reflected that "a reliable source reported that on November 22, 1963, several hours after the assassination of President John F. Kennedy, Luisa Calderon Carralero, a Cuban employee of the Cuban Embassy in Mexico City, and believed to be a member of the Cuban Directorate General of Intelligence (DGI), discussed news of the assassination with an acquaintance," commenting, "Yes, of course, I knew almost before Kennedy." With all of these interesting pieces of evidence in hand, and the intention of personally talking to the consulate employees and hopefully getting an opportunity to question the suspect (Fidel Castro) himself, Louis Stokes (the Select Committee's Chairman), Richardson Preyer (the Chairman of the Kennedy Subcommittee), Bob Blakey (the Committee's Chief Counsel), Eddie Lopez (one of our brightest staff researchers, who had spent some months reading the CIA's classified files on Cuba, including the files about Oswald's visit to the Cuban Consulate), and I went to Cuba.

We were able to spend several days in Cuba, and just being able to see Cuba firsthand was perhaps as informative as asking questions. The assistance given to us by the Cuban government was (at least on the surface) more friendly and cooperative than what we received from our own FBI and CIA. They gave us documents that we requested, allowed us to interview a number of their citizens (with the exception of Luisa Calderon, who was reportedly ill, but who did respond to written questions that we submitted), and allowed their two previous consuls in Mexico City, Eusebio Azcue and Alfredo Mirabal, to not only talk to us, but come to Washington and testify in our public hearings.

We were housed in a nice, remotely located home in the countryside, a hundred yards or so off of one of Cuba's spectacularly beautiful, white sand beaches. Each day, a fleet of four black 1960 Ford Falcons picked us up and took us to the interviews, and also for sightseeing trips. The Ford Falcons (the official fleet of government limousines), as well as every other car that we saw on the streets in Cuba (all of which were of the same vintage as the Falcons), looked like they came out of an antique car show — completely new, inside and out. It gave you the sense that you had been transported back in time, or perhaps, that all clocks had simply stopped when relations between Cuba and the U.S. were broken at the end of 1960, and Cuba's access to everything American dried up.

Our tour guide and interpreter was a beautiful, young Cuban woman (who, reportedly, was Castro's mistress). In the house on the beach, there was a gentle looking, older lady who supervised a small staff that catered to our every need. Everyone was so nice and friendly. But below the facade was the other Cuba.

For the first day or so, the motorcade of black Ford Falcons drove us everywhere at a very high rate of speed, even down the narrow alleys that were barely wide enough to allow the small cars to pass between the buildings. I jokingly said to the driver of the car I was in (in my get-by Spanish) that I really liked the way they drove in Cuba, it was *fast,* just the way that I drove in the United States. The driver laughed. Then, the next day, the motorcade went slowly. I asked what had caused the change in style, and my driver said that he had told his superior what I had said, and that the superior thought I was being critical, so he commanded the drivers to slow down. The next day, things were back to normal, down the narrow alleys at 50 miles per hour. I again inquired, and was told that the immediate superior's order had been over-turned by higher authority: "We were told that we must drive fast, for security reasons." The full story came out. Speed was necessary to protect the motorcade from being attacked.

The beautiful country home soon gave up some of its secrets too. Each bedroom had its own antique radio (right out of the 1950's). One evening, when it was turned off, I heard muffled voices coming from the other end of the wires. The radio was not just a radio, it was a two-way listening de-vice—our conversations were being secretly monitored! For the rest of the trip, when Blakey and I wanted to talk about the case, we always waited until we could take a walk on beach.

And then there was the morning that I got up unusu-ally early and, as I walked by the kitchen door, saw the sweet little old lady who had been so friendly to us, speaking to a member of the house staff. In a tone of voice that sent shud-ders through me, she was giving military-style instructions to the servant about not getting friendly with the American enemies. I felt a cold chill as I realized that she was no mere housekeeper. The image that came immediately to mind was the scene from that old James Bond movie when a similar, sweet little old lady turned on Bond in a split second Dr. Jeckel-to-Mr. Hyde transformation, and began chasing him around the room attempting to kick him with the needle-sharp poisonous spike that popped out from the toe of her octogenarian-style black lace-up shoe.

The cumulative feeling that came from these events was not fear for my physical safety, but claustrophobia. Within only a few days I had come to feel what it must be like to live in a police state. In the United States we often become concerned or even angry about the size and power of government and the extent of its encroachment into our lives, but we can probably only intellectually conceptualize the problem, and not really feel what it means to live in a country where "Big Brother is always watching you." When I finally got on the plane to return to the United States, I felt as if I were escaping.

In terms of our investigation, the trip to Cuba was nothing less than humbling: it was clear that we had no power to learn anything from Castro's Cuban subjects other than what the Cuban government wanted us to learn. The Cuban citizens we interviewed appeared to be—and may have even wanted to be—open and friendly and candid, but Cuba was an eye- opener—even for a criminal prosecutor— about how misleading demeanor can be.

On the last afternoon of the trip, we still did not know

if we would be permitted to question Castro. Then, word came that the premier would be available. We were taken to a modern building where Castro's office was located, and escorted into a conference room and given banana daiquiris while we waited. Then the time came. We were taken to Castro's office. Castro, our tour guide and interpreter, and two men from the Cuban DGI (similar to our CIA) were present. As we entered his office, photographers took everyone's picture shaking hands with Castro.

The office was extremely contemporary in style, large and rectangular in shape, with high ceilings and a glass wall overlooking the city. Castro's desk, table-style without drawers below, was in one corner, with bookcases on the wood-paneled wall behind it. Everyone was seated around a large, thick, irregularly shaped, black marble coffee table, that had rough cut edges and a polished top and rested on a grass rug. Around the marble table were chairs and a couch, all covered in cow hide with the hair left on. On the brick wall, behind the couch where Castro and the interpreter sat, was a large painting that I at first thought was simply a swirl of colors, but then recognized as a portrait of Castro's long-time friend, Che Guevara.

Castro was dressed in his traditional army fatigues, and sat casually with one foot tucked up under his other leg. Everyone was offered one of Castro's personal, hand-rolled Cohiba cigars (which, as I recall, only I accepted). Castro answered our questions in a free flowing, animated style, gesturing with his hands and explaining his rationales in a demeanor that appeared quite credible. Although he spoke in Spanish, there were no pauses for translations. Instead, the interpreter translated simultaneously, and the questions and answers flowed so smoothly that the language difference was not even noticeable.

Castro denied that Oswald made any threats in the presence of Cuban consulate employees during his trip to Mexico City in September, 1963. Castro also denied ever personally speaking to Comer Clark. Castro took the position that if any such threat had been made, the Cuban government would have been morally obligated to report it to the United States.

On the issue of whether he (i.e., Cuba) had been involved in the assassination, Castro said:

> That [the Cuban Government might have been involved in the President's death] was insane. From the ideological point of view it was insane. And from the political point of view, it was a tremendous insanity. I am going to tell you here that nobody ever had the idea of such things. What would it do? We just tried to defend our folks here, within our territory. Anyone who subscribed to that idea would have been judged insane . . . absolutely sick. Never, in 20 years of revolution, I never heard anyone suggest nor even speculate about a measure of that sort, because who could think of the idea of organizing the death of the President of the United States. That would have been the most perfect pretext for the United States to invade our country which is what I have tried to

prevent for all these years, in every possible sense. Since the United States is much more powerful than we are, what could we gain from a war with the United States? The United States would lose nothing. The destruction would have been here.

But did Castro know about the CIA/Mafia plots to kill him? In a speech he gave on September 7, 1963, it appeared that he not only knew, but had considered retaliation. Here is what he said about that:

> So, I said something like those plots start to set a very bad precedent, a very serious one—that could become a boomerang against the authors of those actions . . . but I did not mean to threaten by that. I did not mean even that . . . not in the least . . . but rather, like a warning that we knew; that we had news about it; and that to set those precedents of plotting the assassination of leaders of other countries would be a very bad precedent. . . something very negative. And, if at present, the same would happen under the same circumstances, I would have no doubt in saying the same as I said [then] because I didn't mean a threat that we were going to take measures—similar measures—like a retaliation for that. We never meant that because we knew that there were plots. For 3 years, we had known there were plots against us. So the conversation came about very casually, you know; but I would say that all these plots or attempts were part of the everyday life.

On balance, I think we learned something from questioning the suspect, even though it was fifteen years after the crime, and even though it was in his country and he was absolutely free to say whatever he wanted without fear of sanction, and even though the interview did not provide any of the evidentiary detail upon which homicide cases are routinely solved. I personally believe that part of what Castro told us was not the truth—the evidence indicates that Oswald did make threats against the president while talking to Cuban consulate employees in Mexico City in September, 1963—and to the extent that Castro falsely denied that those threats occurred, it is appropriate to consider the common rule of law that false testimony by a suspect permits the jury to draw an inference of consciousness of guilt. But covering up his own guilt was obviously not the only possible explanation for the lie. Another possible reason that Castro would not admit those threats by Oswald is simply that it was more "politically correct" (even if illogical) for him to take the position that if those statements had been made, his government would have had the moral obligation to report them.

On the arguably more important issue, Castro did admit that he knew about the plots to assassinate him. He said that he did not engage in similar activity against Kennedy because the risks for his country were simply too great. You may find his explanation in that regard to be believable simply because, whatever else may be said about him, over the past forty years he has not proven himself to be a stupid or a reckless leader—or, you may not.

Was Lee Harvey Oswald the
real assassin, or was he a patsy?

The ultimate answer to that question is a little complex, so let's begin with the Warren Commission's basic conclusion that Lee Harvey Oswald fired three shots at the presidential limousine from the sixth floor window of the Texas School Book Depository. If Oswald did that, then whatever else he may or may not have been, he was not *simply* a patsy.

The investigation of the narrow issue of whether Oswald fired at the presidential limousine that was done by the Warren Commission and the FBI in 1963–64, even though flawed in some significant respects, was aggressively pursued, and it developed a large body of evidence supporting the Warren Commission's conclusion. The conclusion does not rest upon any one decisive piece of evidence. Instead it rests upon an array of evidence.

From the available evidence, it appears that Oswald purchased the Mannlicher-Carcano rifle that was found on the sixth floor of the Texas School Book Depository immediately after the assassination (indicated in part by his handwriting on the order form); that he subsequently possessed the rifle (indicated in part by photos of him taken by his wife showing him holding the rifle, including one such photo that he signed his name on the back of, and gave to a friend, and also indicated by his palm print on the rifle that was recovered from the sixth floor after the shooting); that he was an employee of the School Book Depository and was seen in the building shortly before and immediately after the assassination; that the boxes near the sixth floor window which apparently were arranged to create "the sniper's nest" bore his palm print and his fingerprint; that it was Oswald's Mannlicher-Carcano that fired the fatal bullets (indicated by traditional "ballistics" tests showing that the three shell casings found near the sixth floor Book Depository window had been fired in that rifle and that two bullet fragments found in the limousine and one recovered from Governor Connally's stretcher in the hospital had been fired from that rifle, and by neutron activation analysis conducted by the Select Committee indicating that the bullet fragments found in the limousine and recovered from Governor Connally's wrist were probably bits and pieces of Mannlicher-Carcano bullets); and that shots came from the general vicinity of that same sixth floor window (indicated by "trajectory analysis" based upon photographic and medical data of the location of

41

wounds suffered by the president and Governor John Connally, some eyewitness accounts including employees who were watching the motorcade from the 5th floor directly below the sixth floor window, and scientific acoustics testing of sound patterns on the Dallas Police Department dispatch tape recording). Finally, the evidence indicated that Oswald fled the School Book Depository building immediately after the assassination; killed a police officer (J. D. Tippit) approximately 45 minutes later (documented by both eyewitness testimony and ballistics data showing that the shell casings found at the site of Tippit's death were fired from the pistol taken from Oswald when he was arrested shortly after Tippit's murder); resisted arrest; lied about owning the Mannlicher-Carcano rifle; and falsely claimed that his head had been superimposed on someone else's body in the backyard photos that appeared to show him holding the rifle.

Now if you have read any book or newspaper article or seen anything television show about the Kennedy case before now, you already know that every single piece of evidence implicating Oswald as having shot at the president has been challenged, questioned and even ridiculed over time. But what you may not know is that nearly all of the prominent theories for rejecting the evidence about Oswald having fired at the limousine arose in the first dozen years after the assassination, and the bases underlying those theories were tested by panels of experts employed by the Select Committee on Assassinations. For example, our photographic experts examined the photographic evidence to see if the photos of Oswald holding the rifle had been altered (e.g., to see if they contained evidence that Oswald's head had really been superimposed on someone else's body), and to see if the rifle in the pictures had sufficient unique markings to really say that it was the same rifle that was taken from the sixth floor after the shooting. In addition, the Select Committee's panels of experts also re-examined the basic evidence: re-did the ballistics tests, re-examined the handwritings which were allegedly Oswald's, re-did the fingerprint examinations, and conducted neutron activation analysis on the bullet fragments found in the limousine (bombarding the lead fragments with neutrons, to determine each fragment's precise metallic composition, and thereby how many bullets the fragments came from).

In the end, the overall body of evidence clearly pointed to the conclusion that Oswald fired his own rifle at the presidential limousine as it passed beneath the window of his place of employment. That explanation, at least, best takes into account and is consistent with the majority of the credible evidence. Further, there has never been any significant body of credible reasons to reject this conclusion, although there certainly have been a large number of misconceptions and misunderstandings that have led many people to question it.

Many questions about this conclusion initially arose for very legitimate reasons. Many questions arose from the fact that a number of significant blunders were made during the course of the original autopsy, including descriptions of location of bullet wounds in the president; and from the Warren Commission's decision (apparently based, at least in part, upon the rationale of "preserving the Kennedy family's desires for privacy") not to independently review either the autopsy x-rays or the autopsy photographs, nor to make those photos or x-rays publicly available, nor to show them to any independent panel of experts (which would have revealed that in significant respects the clinical pathologists who performed the autopsy had not done a competent job). Other questions arose from the fact that some highly relevant evidence was destroyed during the 1963–64 investigation (including such things as the original autopsy notes of the chief pathologist, and the record of a pre-assassination contact with Oswald by the FBI).

Once it became rather clear that the Warren Commission's investigative procedures and some of its principal conclusions could not be trusted, then the Warren Commission itself was not trusted, and all of its conclusions were challenged. But given the complexity of the events and the huge quantity of available evidence, getting real answers to fill the credibility void left by the Warren Commission has never been easy. Realistically, it is difficult in any criminal case, and impossible in a case such as the Kennedy case, to properly evaluate the evidence without investigative powers (including the power to compel the production of documents and witnesses), a lot of money (to hire experts, investigators, and researchers), and a lot of time, expertise and training to evaluate the evidence. Such a combination of tools is usually only available through a massive government investigation, and that combination of tools has been focused upon the Kennedy case on only one occasion since 1964.

When we applied such resources to the task between 1977 and 1979, we confirmed that much of what the Warren Commission said was wrong. But we also found that most of the many reasons that led critics of the Warren Commission to conclude that Oswald was a mere patsy were also wrong, and were based upon inadequate access to the available evidence, questionable assumptions and logic, and/or faulty "scientific" analysis. Since 1979, when the Select Committee published its findings, many of the earlier misunderstandings have unfortunately persisted because those who have had the time and resources to thoroughly study the evidence and to present it to the public, apparently have had other agendas. To see if you agree with our findings, let's look in detail at some of the evidence and the theories that have challenged it.

How many bullets were fired,
and from where?

The answer to this question does not end, but it perhaps begins with Chapter III of the Warren Commission's 1964 Report, which they styled, "The Shots From the Texas School Book Depository." Therein, the Warren Commission set forth its conclusion that three shots were fired, all from the sixth floor of the Texas School Book Depository. Eye witness accounts as to the number and origin of the shots were conflicting, ranging from two to as many as five or six shots originating from various locations, principally the School Book Depository and the "grassy knoll" or picket fence area that is just west of the School Book building. The physical evidence included various still photos, and also three motion pictures provided by spectators Orville Nix, Mary Muchmore, and Abraham Zapruder.

The Warren Commission also had evidence that both the Mannlicher-Carcano rifle and three spent shell casings which had been fired in and ejected from it, were found on the sixth floor of the School Book building minutes after the shooting. No other weapon was found. No other shell casings were found.

And the Warren Commission had the president's body (or more particularly, the autopsy report) and his clothing (coat, shirt and tie) from which they concluded that one bullet entered the president's upper back (although they usually described it as entering the lower part of his neck) and exited his throat, and another bullet entered his head from the rear and caused a massive head wound. They also had medical data (and clothing) showing that Governor John Connally, who was seated in the presidential limousine on a jump seat in front of the president, suffered wounds from a bullet that entered his back and exited his chest, a wound from a bullet that pierced his right wrist, and a puncture wound in his left thigh. A "nearly whole bullet" (the Warren Commission's description) that reportedly fell off of the stretcher that carried Governor Connally into Parkland Hospital, presumably had dislodged from the puncture wound in his thigh. And finally, the nose portion of a bullet was found on the front seat of the limousine beside the driver, the base portion of a bullet was found on the right side of the front passenger seat, three small lead fragments were found on the carpet under the left jump seat (where Mrs. Connally was seated), there was a dent on the inside of the strip of chrome across the top of the limousine's windshield just to the left of the rear view mirror (which appeared too small to have been caused by a direct hit from full bullet, but may have been caused by a fragment of a bullet traveling at high speed), and a small lead fragment (that left a lead smear) appeared to have hit the inside of windshield. The total combined weight of the lead fragments found in the limousine was less than the weight of a whole Mannlicher-Carcano bullet, and thus all of the fragments could have come from either one bullet, or more than one bullet.

Finally, the Warren Commission performed "wounds ballistics" tests, which showed what a rather heavy, relatively slow moving (muzzle velocity of less than 200 feet per second), fully jacketed Mannlicher-Carcano bullet tended to do in terms of tissue damage, bullet deformation, and reduction in velocity and direction, when traveling through various type of body tissue—soft muscle, boney wrists, skulls, etc.

The Warren Commission concluded from this evidence that there were only three shots, namely the three bullets that would have come from the three spent shell cases found on the sixth floor of the Book Depository. Based upon the testimony of firearms experts, the Commission found that the unique, microscopic markings (random patterns) on the three spent rifle cartridges, as well as on the two large bullet pieces found on the front seat of the limousine and the whole bullet found on Connally's stretcher, proved that the casings, the fragments and the whole bullet were all fired in the Mannlicher-Carcano that was found on the sixth floor.

The Warren Commission recounted in detail the principal witness accounts that a rifle was seen protruding from, and that shots were fired from the sixth floor window. The Warren Commission rejected all eyewitness accounts of there being more than three shots, and all eyewitness accounts of a shot or shots coming from another location, stating that "No credible evidence suggests that the shots were fired from the railroad bridge over the Triple Underpass, the nearby railroad yards or any place other than the Texas School Book Depository Building." The justification for these wholesale credibility distinctions—everyone who heard three shots from the Book Depository was credible, everyone else was not—was arguably that no physical evidence was found to corroborate the accounts of shots from other locations. (Perhaps, it was also because to credit those accounts would have indicated a second shooter in addition to the one who was apprehended, but that is another story.)

Following along with the Warren Commission's analysis, if one of Oswald's three shots hit the president in the head, the next question is, Where did the other two shots go?

The "Single Bullet" Theory

The Warren Commission ultimately concluded that one of Oswald's other shots missed everything, and the other one hit both Kennedy and Connally, causing the back and neck wounds in Kennedy, and the back, chest, wrist and thigh wounds in Connally. This theory, known as "the single

49

bullet theory," has been one of the principal causes of public distrust in the conclusion that Oswald's bullets killed the president.

The "single bullet" conclusion arose from the Warren Commission's review of the evidence described above, together with an attempted reconstruction of the timing of the shots. One of the principal tools they used for that attempted reconstruction was the Zapruder film.

The Zapruder film was the most comprehensive of the films taken at the time of the assassination. It was made by Abraham Zapruder, a manufacturer of ladies dresses in Dallas, who used his home movie camera to film the motorcade while he stood on a concrete abutment between the Book Depository and the grassy knoll. The Zapruder film shows the presidential limousine from the point where it turned the corner onto Elm Street in front of the School Book Depository, until after it passed by the grassy knoll and entered the triple underpass—thus covering the entire period of time from before any shots were fired until after a bullet struck the president in the head—with the sole exception of slightly more than a second when the limousine was hidden from Zapruder's view by the Stemmons Freeway sign.

Because the Zapruder film provides the best continuous photographic account of the assassination, it was used by the Warren Commission (and over the years has remained) as a sort of assassination clock, with all of the visible events, as well as the various assumptions about the timing of shots, being referred to by Zapruder film frame numbers. The "frame numbers" are not actually on the film, but were originally assigned by the Warren Commission, with the number "1" given to the first frame where the motorcycles leading the motorcade first came into Zapruder's view on Houston Street. Because the film ran at 18.3 frames per second, the timing of events can be accurately inferred from the number of elapsed frames. Using this numbering method, Zapruder frame 312 contains the sight of Kennedy being hit in the head. The entire film is just short of 500 frames in length.

Because Zapruder was using simply a home movie camera, the film did not run fast enough to visually record any bullet in flight, or the impact of any shot other than the shot that exploded Kennedy's head. It was clear from the "reactions" of both the president and Governor Connally (who was seated in front of the president) that they had both been struck by another bullet, or bullets, prior to Kennedy being struck in the head, but exactly when a bullet or bullets *struck* in relation to the *reactions* that can be seen in the film, is uncertain.

Nor did the Zapruder film record sound (as our modern day home video cameras do). Because the earlier shots cannot be directly seen or heard, the timing of the shots that preceded the head shot cannot be directly determined from the Zapruder film. Over the years, there have been many conflicting conclusions as to what can legitimately be "inferred" from the film as to when the earlier bullet (or bullets) may have struck the president and Governor.

Finally, it is important to recognize that Mr. Zapruder

was viewing the motorcade from the north side of Elm street, west of the School Book Depository, so his view was quite different than the view from the sixth floor window of the Book Depository. Between approximately frames 200 and 225, Zapruder's view of the limousine was blocked by the Stemmons Freeway sign, but that sign did not block the view from the sixth floor. The Warren Commission concluded in its attempted "reconstruction" that between approximately frames 166 and 210, the foliage of a large oak tree partially blocked the view of the limousine from the sixth floor, but that tree never blocked Zapruder's view. During their reconstruction, the Warren Commission (actually, the FBI) filmed from the sixth floor the views that they believed a shooter would have had as the limousine passed below, and included photos of those views as Commission exhibits in their final Report, labeled to reflect the corresponding Zapruder frames numbers.

The Warren Commission's analysis which produced the single bullet conclusion was described in a section of their Report entitled "The Trajectory." That analysis was based upon a number of debatable assumptions, including assumptions about what could be inferred from Kennedy's and Connally's apparent "reactions" to being hit (i.e., what the Warren Commission could see in the Zapruder film); the assumption that, in firing at the limousine, Oswald used the telescopic sight on the rifle; assumptions about (and reliance upon) tests showing how long it would have taken him to fire, reload and fire again *if* he was using the scope; assumptions about what could be seen through the scope and thus when he would have fired in relation to the oak tree foliage that partially blocked his view for approximately 2.4 seconds; and assumptions about the ability of eyewitnesses to discern with precision the delay between the sounds of shots and reactions to wounds.

Using such assumptions, the Warren Commission first concluded that "Tests of the assassin's rifle disclosed that at least 2.3 seconds were required between shots." The Warren Commission next concluded that the first shot that hit occurred between Zapruder frames 210 and 225:

> It is probable that the President was not shot before frame 210, since it is unlikely that the assassin would deliberately have shot at him with a view obstructed by the oak tree when he was about to have a clear opportunity. It is also doubtful that even the most proficient marksman would have hit him through the oak tree. In addition, the President's reaction is 'barely apparent' in frame 225, which is 15 frames or approximately eight-tenths second after frame 210, and a shot much before 210 would assume a longer reaction time than was recalled by eyewitnesses at the scene.

(I particularly like the reasoning that eyewitnesses at the scene could have distinguished between a "visible" reaction delay of 8/10 of a second after they heard a shot, as compared to a reaction delay of, say, 1.6 seconds! How many traumatic events in your life do you think you could describe the timing of with that amount of precision? But the reasoning suited their conclusion, so the Warren Commission went with it.)

For reasons that I will describe in greater detail below, those conclusions can be questioned not only because of their underlying assumptions, but upon the basis of subsequently developed evidence. However, there was one part of the Warren Commission's analysis that did not rely upon a lot of debatable assumptions, and instead rested more directly upon the basic evidence:

> According to Special Agent Robert A. Frazier, who occupied the position of the assassin in the sixth-floor window during the re-enactment, it is likely that the bullet which passed through the President's neck, as described previously, then struck the automobile or someone else in the automobile. The minute examination by the FBI inspection team, conducted in Washington between 14 and 16 hours after the assassination, revealed no damage indicating that a bullet struck any part of the interior of the Presidential limousine, with the exception of the cracking of the windshield and the dent on the windshield chrome. Neither of these points of damage to the car could have been caused by the bullet which exited from the President's neck at a velocity of 1,772 to 1,779 feet per second. If the trajectory had permitted the bullet to strike the windshield, the bullet would have penetrated it and traveled a substantial distance down the road unless it struck some other object en route. Had that bullet struck the metal framing, which was dented, it would have torn a hole in the chrome and penetrated the framing, both

inside and outside the car. At that exit velocity, the bullet would have penetrated any other metal or upholstery surface of the interior of the automobile.

The bullet that hit President Kennedy in the back and exited through his throat most likely could not have missed both the automobile and its occupants. Since it did not hit the automobile, Frazier testified that it probably struck Governor Connally. The relative positions of President Kennedy and Governor Connally at the time when the President was struck in the neck confirm that the same bullet probably passed through both men.

Thus, the conclusion that a single bullet went through both Connally and Kennedy was based upon the physical evidence indicating that three shots were fired from the sixth floor of the Book Depository, wounds ballistics testing (showing how fully-jacketed Mannlicher-Carcano bullets tend to act), photographic and medical data indicating the approximate alignment of Kennedy and Connally's bodies and of their wounds, and perhaps most importantly, upon the absence of an apparent alternative explanation about where the bullet that hit Kennedy in the neck would have gone if it did not go through Connally, i.e., the absence of evidence of other damage to the interior of the limousine. If the bullet was gradually slowed down by going through Kennedy's neck, then Connally's chest, then Connally's wrist, and it finally stopped in Connally's thigh (ultimately being recovered from his stretcher in the hospital), it would have created no damage to the car. If it somehow missed Connally, where did it hit the car? If Oswald fired the bullet from the sixth floor window that hit Kennedy in the upper back, the basic flight path was *down* into the limousine. If the bullet (that medical evidence showed hit from the rear) was fired from some other location, i.e., from some location that would have allowed it to go through Kennedy and then miss both the limousine interior and the other occupants, the Warren Commission, at least, found no evidence—no other weapon, no other bullet jackets, no other lead fragments—evidencing any such firing.

The Warren Commission's final conclusion, of course, was that Oswald's other shot simply missed everything. (In one of its rare admissions that it simply did not know, the Commission said that it could not be determined whether the shot that missed was Oswald's first, second, or third shot.)

The Zapruder film, and Reaction Analysis

The "single bullet" theory has been questioned on many grounds, each of which has its own set of underlying assumptions. In part, questions have arisen from the same kind of Zapruder film "reaction" analysis, and are based on the same kind of questionable underlying assumptions that the Warren Commission used in describing its conclusions in the first place.

From the three shell cases found on the sixth floor of the Texas School Book Depository, the Warren Commission concluded that three shots were fired. If the second or third of the three bullets hit Kennedy in the head, either one or both of the other bullets could have caused the earlier "reactions" visible in the Zapruder film. In attempting to determine what happened, the Warren Commission used various assumptions about what Oswald would and would not have done, and about what inferences could be drawn from "reactions" of the limousine's occupants. Using such assumptions, the Warren Commission concluded that both Kennedy and Connally were shot at some point between Zapruder frames 210 and 240. Some critics of the Warren Commission have postulated it was because of that 30 frame "window" of time that the Warren Commission actually created its single bullet theory in the first place, since if two separate bullets hit within those 30 frames of the film, those bullets were spaced no more than about 1.6 seconds apart, and the FBI (purportedly) had proven that the rifle could not be shot that fast. Thus, these critics say, the single bullet explanation was "concocted" in order to avoid a finding that there were two shooters. Other critics have viewed the Zapruder film (and/or used the Warren Commission's observations about "reactions") and concluded that a single bullet could not have caused the wounds to both Kennedy and Connally because from the film it appears that Connally had no reaction until at least 1/2 a second after Kennedy reacted. From these *apparent* facts (the reactions of Kennedy and Connally) not only many private citizens but some prominent news media have concluded that the photographic evidence alone indicates that Connally and Kennedy were hit at different times, and thus by different bullets, since they *appear* to react at different times in the film.

But are the underlying assumptions necessarily correct? The first (often unspoken) assumption is that we can really see their reactions from the Zapruder film as soon as they were actually "reacting." Other underlying assumptions are that bullet wounds cause pain, and that the film would reflect some significant reaction to that pain. Finally, these conclusions necessarily assume that reaction times to wounds are essentially the same for all people, for all types of wounds, and for wounds to different parts of the body.

I believe that such "assumptions" have always been one of the major problems with much of the "analysis" that has been done of issues in the Kennedy case. Issues are analyzed based upon a myriad of different *assumptions* about physical and psychological phenomena about which we probably know much less than we assume we know. From such assumptions, conclusions are drawn—about Oswald, about conspiracy, about government motives in conducting investigations—without really ever questioning the validity of the underlying assumptions. It is often obvious that we must question the *evidence*; it is often less obvious that we must also question the *assumptions* that we use in evaluating the evidence.

Just as the Warren Commission was too often too quick to justify its conclusions on the basis of questionable assumptions, many of the books and articles written since 1964 include unsupportable inferences and conclusions about what the Zapruder film "shows" or "proves." Most have proceeded on the assumption that because it is a film, it portrays "obvious" truths. If we take the time to look at some of these underlying assumptions in greater detail, what at first blush may seem "obvious" may not be quite so obvious.

The President's Head Jerked Backward

One such commonly asserted "obvious" deduction from the film is that because the Zapruder film shows that President Kennedy's head jerks *backward* when it was struck by a bullet, that means that he was struck by a bullet from the *front*. That may at first seem like a reasonable or even obvious conclusion, but our wounds ballistics experts shot goats from the *rear*, and demonstrated that their heads jerked *backward*, as a result of a nervous or muscular contraction. Tests have even indicated that when a watermelon is shot, causing it to explode, a portion of it will move backward (toward the direction of the gun) as a result of the explosion, instead of forward from the force of the bullet (as might be expected).

Is what we see *reality*, or what we *want* to see?

The Zapruder film is great evidence, but it is not a consistently *clear* film. Mr. Zapruder tried to photograph a moving motorcade with a home movie camera. The film wasn't made with modern day, professional quality equipment, nor taken by a professional photographer.

Because it was not a high speed camera, any quick or erratic movements by Mr. Zapruder or the subjects being filmed caused the images of the moving limousine and its occupants to be unclear—parts of it are blurry at best. The Committee did use computer digital enhancement techniques to improve its clarity, and such techniques have been applied more recently by private parties, but (at least to date) significant numbers of frames have always lacked clarity and detail. (Because it contains periodic increased blurriness—some frames are clear, some are not—the Select Committee even had its photographic panel study the periodic increases in blurriness to see if any inferences could be drawn based upon the possibility that the shock wave of bullets and/or Zapruder's reactions to loud sounds may have had a jarring effect. It was an interesting, but inherently inconclusive exercise, again due to the limitations implicit in the underlying assumptions.)

The fuzziness of portions of the film does seem to have at least one "advantage," that of giving each person who views the film a little bit of "artistic license" to see whatever they want to see! The more that people have searched the blurry images for hidden detail, the more "information" they have often found. But often, as where some believed that they could see evidence in the film that the Secret Service agent in the front seat of the limousine had shot the president with his revolver, subsequent analysis has revealed that suspicious looking flashes of light were simply flashes of reflected light.

In their attempt to extract detail from the film, the Warren Commission concluded that Kennedy's first visible reaction to being hit was at frame 225; the Select Committee's experts believed the first visible reaction was around frames 200–207. Governor Connally viewed the film, and told the Warren Commission he believed he was hit around frames 233–235, and books and magazine articles over the years have often concluded that Connally's first visible reaction is at frame 233. The Select Committee's experts believed that a noticeable reaction by Connally could be seen at frames 222–226.

My point is not to deny that the Zapruder film is one of the best pieces of photographic evidence that is available, but simply to suggest that it can be either a valuable or a misleading piece in recreating the puzzle of what happened. Unfortunately, the Zapruder film, like so much of the evidence in the Kennedy case, has as often been a source of illusion as of illumination.

Can't you tell from Kennedy's and Connally's "reactions" when the bullets were fired?

All day long, everyday, we draw inferences or conclusions from the "data" that confronts us—from what we see, from words spoken to us, from events described in the news. Our inferences or conclusions from such "data" are often based upon some personal experience that we have had, or some event that we have personally observed previously in our lives. But because our personal experiences are necessarily limited, they can be very misleading.

We take out a kitchen knife and start to slice an apple; we cut our finger; it hurts; we react (with arm movements, facial expressions, and perhaps verbal obscenities). Usually, it doesn't take very long to react. From that we assume that Kennedy and Connally would have immediately reacted, as soon as they were hit by bullets. After all, isn't being shot even worse than cutting your finger?

Getting shot may be worse, but can we predict that reactions to it would really be the same as what we experienced in the kitchen? Fortunately for humanity, but unfortunately for scientific analysis, there really isn't a lot of scientifically recorded evidence in the form of photographs of people being shot under controlled circumstances, in which bullet impact can be compared to visible reaction. But there may be analogies more helpful than the finger-cut analogy we started with.

Here is my own "assumption," based on my own experience. Excluding the shot to Kennedy's head, which vividly shows the moment of bullet impact as a gaping wound explodes his head, brain matter is visibly blown into the air, and "reaction" and "impact" are thus virtually simultaneous, my belief is that the timing of shots cannot be inferred from what we can see in the film of Kennedy's and Connally's reactions, since the time relationship between bullet *impact* and *reactions* to being struck cannot be known. I further believe that their individual reactions not only could have been delayed for some seconds after they were hit, but also that each of their reactions could have been delayed for quite different periods of time.

I base these beliefs upon a traumatic injury that I had some years ago—a water skiing accident. Not paying close attention to the location of the boat, I looked up while making a wide and fast turn to the outside of the wake to discover that a rocky shoreline was directly in front of me. I was probably traveling over 40 miles an hour, too fast at least to stop, so I kicked off the ski and went into a roll which took me through some brush and stumps in the shallow water and onto the rocky shoreline. When I came up, I was sitting in only a few inches of water, and felt a large glob of something on my face. I immediately assumed that I had gouged out my eye (although I felt no pain). I covered my other eye with my hand, and was relieved to find out that I could still see out of the eye that I feared was laying on my cheek. Some seconds later, the boat got back to me, and I was confronted with the anguished looks of everyone in the boat staring at my face. I climbed into the boat, rode to the location where we had parked the car, got out of the boat and walked to the car. When seated in the car, I looked in the passenger vanity mirror. I then discovered that the large blob on my cheek was my eyebrow, eye lid, and a large part of my face, which I had torn off on some underwater obstruction while I was rolling through the shallow water toward shore. That side of my face was simply bone with an eye. Even when I looked in the mirror, I still felt no pain.

We drove to the nearest hospital, I got out and walked to the emergency room, and lay down on a stretcher. I still had felt no pain, but at that point I began to go into shock. Over the next hours, a plastic surgeon reconstructed my face, and after a couple of days, I was released from the hospital. *But it was weeks until I could walk again.* As it turned out, my most serious and painful injury was a large hole that I had torn in my hip, undoubtedly punctured by one of the underwater stumps. The wound was so large and deep that the doctors inserted a tube to allow it to drain and slowly heal from the bottom of the wound outward. My hip was so painful that it took days before I could walk even with crutches, yet immediately after the accident I had climbed into the boat, walked to the car, and walked into the hospital without ever even knowing that I had injured the hip. I first discovered the injury to my hip when I awoke in the hospital the day after the accident.

How long does it take for someone to realize a severe, traumatic injury—especially one that you were not expecting? Does your body save you from the initial shock? Clearly, the Zapruder film shows Kennedy and Connally reacting to their wounds, Kennedy grasping for his neck, and Connally grimacing in pain. But we clearly cannot see the actual impact of any bullet or bullets other than the one that exploded President Kennedy's skull. Just as clearly, the precise frames of the film when their visible reactions begin has and always will be a subject of legitimate debate. And most importantly, how long prior to those *visible* reactions they

64

were actually struck by a bullet or bullets can never be determined from the Zapruder film—no matter how much analysis we do of it.

Many people have suggested many answers to the Kennedy case based upon what they see, or believe they see in the Zapruder film, but can any *real answers* about the number or timing of bullet impacts be derived solely from the Zapruder film? What have masqueraded as answers have often not been real answers, but only a reflection of our not-too-well-thought-out views of the world and how it works. Because so much of the Kennedy folk lore has failed to question the underlying assumptions, the result has been a distorted analysis of the issues, and relatively few rational conclusions about what really happened on November 22, 1963.

The "Magic Bullet" Theory

The movie *JFK*, by Oliver Stone, displayed another prominent reason that has historically been cited as a basis for rejecting the conclusion that Oswald fired the shots that killed the president, the so-called "magic bullet" theory (an obvious mocking of the Warren Commission's "single bullet theory"). You may recall the trial scene in the movie wherein District Attorney Jim Garrison, played by Kevin Costner, in arguments to the jury, ridiculed the Warren Commission's explanation of how a single bullet from Oswald's gun was able to pass through the bodies of both Kennedy and Governor John Connally. Costner demonstrated an allegedly circuitous route that the bullet would have had to take if the Warren Commission's data were to be believed, diagraming abrupt changes in direction that obviously a high speed rifle bullet could not have made. The ultimate point, of course, was that the Warren Commission's explanation was so patently ridiculous that it actually constituted proof of a government conspiracy to deliberately lie to the public and coverup the government's own complicity.

But does the single bullet theory actually require a circuitous bullet path through the two bodies? In the movie, at least, the body alignment of the two "passengers" used to demonstrate the alleged circuitous route paid no attention to available evidence indicating how the bodies were actually positioned in the limousine, and the trial staging actually exaggerated the body alignments to make the route seem as circuitous as possible. Furthermore, there is no film that shows precisely how Connally and Kennedy were positioned at the time they were struck. The Warren Commission assumed that their alignment should be determined from their apparent positions during Zapruder frames 210–240. Evidence developed by the Select Committee indicated that the first two shots from the Book Depository occurred much earlier, most likely at approximately frames 166 and 186. And various other films of the entire motorcade route show that both Connally and Kennedy moved around considerably, and often quickly, during the course of their ride, sitting up straight, bending forward, and twisting and turning from side to side. (The Warren Commission's assertion that a back brace worn by Kennedy, and the jump seat in which Connally sat, required both of them to sit up straight, was simply wrong.) You can certainly assume positions (as was done in *JFK*) that would require a circuitous route, but you can also assume thousands of other facts if you are willing to do so without concrete evidence, and simply want to postulate hypothetical conspiracy theories.

The "magic bullet" criticisms initially arose, at least in part, from the Warren Commission's inaccurate and conflicting data concerning the location of the bullet wounds suffered by Kennedy and Connally, coupled with the secrecy that for years surrounded the actual autopsy data. There were incorrect and conflicting reports from doctors at Parkland Hospital who tried to save the president, as well as erroneous autopsy findings that arose from the unfortunate political decision to have prestigious *clinical* pathologists conduct the original autopsy of the president. Much speculation and many conspiracy theories have arisen over the years—not only the "magic bullet theory"—based upon the many blunders and inaccurate statements and testimony by the original treating physicians and autopsy doctors.

Clinical pathologists are doctors whose training and experience is in determining the cause of non- violent deaths (often, patients who die in their sleep during the course of hospital treatment for terminal illnesses). The clinical pathologists who performed the autopsy on President Kennedy in 1963 were not experienced in determining the cause of death from a gun shot wound, and did not really know what to look for or how to accurately record what they saw. Such errors in all probability would not have been made by qualified *forensic* pathologists. Unlike clinical pathologists, forensic pathologists are trained and experienced in determining the cause of violent and suspicious deaths, and in testifying about their findings in courts of law where the accuracy of observations and findings are routinely challenged and tested by cross-examination.

Here is what our panel of forensic pathologists had to say about the original autopsy:

> Despite allegations that the Kennedy family or other authorities ordered a partial or limited autopsy, evidence shows that the pathologists were given authority to perform a complete autopsy. The autopsy was not complete, however, according to established medicolegal standards. A combination of strong Kennedy family desires to finish the autopsy quickly, a military environment that hindered independent action, a lack of experience in forensic pathology among the prosecutors, and a lack of established jurisdictional and procedural guidelines all contributed to the pathologists' failure to take certain measures essential to the completion of a thorough medicolegal autopsy and to competently perform the autopsy.

Prominent among the specific failures that resulted from lack of forensic training and expertise, the Bethesda naval doctors failed to record precisely the locations of the wounds according to anatomical landmarks routinely used in forensic pathology, and the reference points they did use to document the location of the wound in the upper back—the mastoid process and the acromion—are *movable* points and simply should not have been used. The Select Committee's forensic pathologists also noted that the Bethesda pathologists' failure to dissect the back wound to determine its track was clearly improper, and that their having merely "probed" the wound with their finger was clearly insufficient to determine the track of the bullet.

In what (at least in other contexts) might be described as a comedy of errors, the Parkland Hospital doctors in Dallas never even observed the entry wound in the president's back, nor the entry wound in the back of his head, and wrongly assumed that the front wound was the entrance. One even speculated at a press conference that the bullet could have entered the throat, been deflected by the spine, and exited (while causing) the head wound! And the Bethesda pathologists never realized that the Dallas doctors had performed a tracheotomy over the exit wound in the president's throat, thereby obliterating essentially all evidence of the exit wound, until the day after they had concluded the autopsy. During the course of the actual autopsy, the Bethesda pathologists wondered if the bullet that entered the president's upper back had perhaps never exited his body, since they did not see any exit wound!

Given the improper procedures, and inaccurate, inconsistent and misleading reports and testimony of the Dallas and Bethesda doctors, it is no wonder that the Warren Commission's "single bullet" conclusion—as well as most of their other findings about bullets and trajectories—has been disbelieved by many who have studied the case. Further, depending upon whose inaccurate report is chosen, it is possible to find "evidence" for any number of different "magical" routes for bullets.

Fortunately, the Select Committee was able, in large part, to redo the autopsy. This fortuity resulted from the fact that there was a photographer present during the original autopsy who took numerous, repetitive photographs during the course of the autopsy. When we placed those photos side-by-side, we were able to view them through 3-D glasses, see what the actual wounds looked like, and better determine their true location. We still could not, however, determine the locations of the soft-tissue wounds with great precision. That was something that should have been and was not done when there was a body that could be physically examined.

The Select Committee's panel was able to determine that the first bullet that struck the president entered his upper back, approximately 5 centimeters below the shoulder and 5 centimeters to the right of the midline of the back. The precise location could not be determined because the original autopsy doctors did not locate it with reference to fixed body landmarks and did not dissect the bullet's track through the body. Nor could our panel reach a definitive decision as to whether this wound, by itself, would have killed the president, although it is possible that he would have died from this wound alone. The precise location of the exit of that hit also could not be determined with precision for similar reasons, although some evidence of it seemed to be visible at the lower edge of the tracheotomy.

Due to available x-rays (which, incidentally, the original pathologists never saw) and the presence of observable skull fractures, the Select Committee's panel was able to locate with precision the point of impact of the second bullet that struck the president. This bullet entered the president's head 10 centimeters above the external occipital protuberance and slightly to the right of the midline, near the upper convexity of the back of the head at the "cowlick" portion of the president's hair part. This entry location was approximately four inches higher than had been reflected in the original autopsy report of the Bethesda doctors! Although the bullet fragmented upon impact, our panel concluded that the main core mass probably exited in the top front area of the skull (right frontoparietal portion) adjacent to the coronal suture.

Based upon the work of our panel, I was able to get the main doctor who performed the original autopsy to admit some of his errors during my cross-examination of him in our public hearings—but not without a lot of hair raising resistance from one of the Select Committee's own forensic pathologists. Late on the evening of September 6, 1978, I was working in my office, preparing to cross-exam Captain James J. Humes, M.D., who was scheduled to testify at the committee hearings the following afternoon, live, on national television. After completing his residency in pathology at the Armed Forces Institute of Pathology in 1956, Captain Humes became the chief of anatomic pathology at the National Naval Medical Center in Bethesda, Maryland in 1960, and the director of the laboratories at the National Medical Center in 1961. It was because he held that respected position that he was chosen to be in charge of the autopsy of President Kennedy.

As I prepared for my cross-examination of Captain Humes, and studied in detail the conclusions of our photographic experts and our panel of forensic pathologists, I realized that Captain Humes' errors in conducting the autopsy had been the cause of many misplaced conspiracy theories over the years. And I came to the conclusion that when he had been questioned under oath on prior occasions, Captain Humes had not told the truth about the facts in an apparent attempt to cover up his own mistakes, and that I could prove it!

Around 9:30 p.m., just as I was finishing the outline of my questioning for the next day, one of the doctors on our forensic pathology panel walked by my office door. Feeling what admittedly may have been excessive trial lawyer enthusiasm, I called for the doctor to come in and told him of my intentions: "Humes has been lying all of these years, and I am going to destroy him!" The Committee's doctor replied, "You cannot do that, Humes is a very respected man!" My cavalier response was something to the effect, "What difference does that make, he hasn't been telling the truth, has he?" The conversation ended—without my realizing the note on which it had ended.

The next day, at the end of the lunch hour, as the television camera lights were being turned on for the afternoon session and I was going over my outline of questions in final preparation to cross-examine Dr. Humes, my pathologist came up to the podium and anxiously said that he had to talk to me. I asked him what the problem was and he said he had taken Humes to lunch and told Humes exactly what my questions were going to be, and that Humes was ready to confess that his original autopsy report was wrong! I was furious. Within minutes, I would have to start questioning Humes. I had the terrible sinking feeling that all of the drama that I had structured my questioning to achieve—the extraction of the truth, Perry Mason style—had just been destroyed by the well-meaning efforts of a doctor who had decided to take it upon himself to save his fellow colleague from public embarrassment.

I went with him and met Humes. What he said was accurate, Humes was ready to admit the errors in his prior testimony. I rushed back to the podium and frantically restructured my outline of questions in light of the development.

Dr. Humes' testimony in some respects was not what I had hoped for, but the important point was made: he finally admitted after fourteen years that he had made mistakes. He abandoned his prior testimony that the skull entrance wound was four inches lower than the autopsy photos showed. It was finally clear that he had been wrong in his description of the location of President Kennedy's head wound, and he regretted destroying his original notes, which had only exacerbated the loss of credibility of the Warren Commission's work over the years. He talked about the pressures he was under in 1963, the lack of sleep over that long weekend of November 23–24 when he prepared the final autopsy report, and the fact that he was handicapped by not being able to look at the autopsy photos and x-rays to prepare his original report (as our pathology panel had been able to do). He hoped that things would be done better next time.

In retrospect, I have to admit that the committee's doctor probably had the right attitude. The mistakes of the past were brought to light, which was the real objective. There was no evidence that Dr. Humes intentionally mishandled the original autopsy, or that he was part of any conspiracy. His errors needed to be corrected, but Dr. Humes did not need to be destroyed in cross-examination. It did make me angry that for so many years he had refused to admit his mistakes, and was willing to do so only when he faced the prospect of being humiliated on national television. Then again, Dr. Humes in one sense was also right: the real hope is that we can all learn from our mistakes, so things will be done better the next time—if there is a next time—that our country has to deal with the assassination of a president.

In the end, when the errors committed by the original clinical pathologists as set out in the Warren Commission Report are corrected, and the Warren Commission's alleged "precision" of wound locations and bullet trajectories are recognized as actually being quite imprecise, there is nothing necessarily "magical" about the path of the single bullet.

The "Pristine Bullet" Theory

Another theory that mocks the Warren Commission's single bullet conclusion is the "pristine bullet theory." The "pristine bullet" theory challenges the Warren Commission's single bullet theory by suggesting that the bullet recovered from Governor Connally's stretcher simply could not have traveled through the bodies of both Kennedy and Connally and remained in such "pristine" condition.

It appears that the term "pristine bullet" was actually borrowed from the Warren Commission Report itself, but the Warren Commission used the term simply to describe a bullet whose flight direction and/or speed had not been altered by hitting anything, and because it was still traveling straight and true and at original velocity, would create wounds somewhat different in nature than bullets that had been deflected. ("The Army Wound Ballistics experts conducted tests which proved that the Governor's wrist wound was not caused by a pristine bullet. A bullet is pristine immediately on exiting from a rifle muzzle when it moves in a straight line with a spinning motion and maintains its uniform trajectory, with a minimum of nose surface striking the air through which it passes.") The Warren Commission did not suggest that the bullet found on the stretcher, the bullet of the "single bullet" theory, was pristine.

Let me digress for a moment to note that I have been describing all of these theories as challenges to the proposition that Oswald killed the president, which in one sense they are. Of course, they have also been used as the basis for suggestions of conspiracy. For example, if the "pristine bullet" could not have been the "single bullet" of the Warren Commission's "single bullet theory"—if it is not really the one that the Warren Commission said traveled through the bodies of Kennedy and Connally, if the bullet that was found on Connally's stretcher in the hospital was really "pristine"— then where did that bullet come from? Don't forget, it's microscopic markings indicate that it *was* fired from Oswald's rifle. So, if it was fired from Oswald's rifle, but did *not* travel through Kennedy and Connally, doesn't that mean that someone planted it on the stretcher in order to frame Oswald? Was it planted to document a phony story that Kennedy and Connally were hit by a bullet fired from the Mannlicher-Carcano that was purchased by Oswald and found on the sixth floor of the School Book Depository? Was it a plant to throw suspicion on Oswald, who was merely someone's patsy?

This is what makes the case so interesting. From each piece of evidence, far ranging implications are often possible. Because these "big questions" are so alluring, it is tempting—and many have not resisted the temptation—to rush to conclusions about conspiracies, jumping over and never really thinking about whether the basic, starting assumptions are really correct. The basic assumptions must first be reasonable if any real answers are to be found. The issues are, first, whether the bullet found on the stretcher is really "pristine," and second, whether it could have made the journey postulated by the single bullet theory and remained in the condition it actually is in.

The "pristine bullet" theory perhaps arose from a simple lack of knowledge; from looking at pictures of the bullet found on the stretcher, seeing that it "looks pristine," assuming that all bullets get deformed whenever they hit anything, and jumping to more sinister conclusions from there. Why it has persisted for so many years is another matter. First, if you could see the actual "pristine bullet" (which I have) you would see that it is actually not "pristine" at all, notwithstanding its superficial appearance in some photographs. It is somewhat deformed and scarred: it is *intact,* but certainly not *pristine.* The Warren Commission Report reflects that minute particles of a bullet were found in Connally's chest and wrist, and that this "stretcher bullet" weighed slightly less than a normal Mannlicher-Carcano.

Second, as the Committee's ballistics and firearms experts demonstrated, there is nothing impossible about a Mannlicher-Carcano bullet traveling the alleged route of "the single bullet," and remaining intact and relatively undeformed. The Mannlicher-Carcano fires a relatively slow moving bullet (compared to many modern-day, high powered rifles), and a relatively long, stable and heavy bullet (compared to many rifles that shoot a relatively small bullet at high velocity in order to achieve a flat, long-range trajectory). Bullets that are relatively light weight, and travel at higher speeds are more likely to be deflected from their course, and to suffer greater deformation—even to completely self-destruct—upon impact with even small and insubstantial objects. Slower moving, longer and heavier bullets like the Mannlicher-Carcano are more likely to continue in a relatively straight line after initial impact, to hold together, and to retain their shape after impact.

The Kennedy autopsy data and Governor Connally's medical records revealed that the bullet hit no major bones as it traveled through their bodies, and our testing revealed that a Mannlicher-Carcano bullet, when traveling through such relatively soft tissue, could be expected to be deformed no more than the "magical, pristine" bullet which for so many years has provided one of the principal bases for rejecting the conclusion that Oswald fired the shots that killed the president.

The Gun Can't Be Fired That Fast

One of the most persistent expressions of doubt that I have heard over the years about the Warren Commission's conclusion that Lee Harvey Oswald was the sole assassin is that Oswald simply could not have accomplished "such a feat of marksmanship." As the theory goes, Oswald wasn't a great shot, the gun was old and not very accurate, the scope was defective, and *no one* could fire the gun that fast.

These doubts were portrayed in a scene in the Oliver Stone movie *JFK*, in which New Orleans District Attorney Jim Garrison has decided to reinvestigate the Kennedy case, and Garrison and his assistant are shown in the School Book Depository discussing the miraculous feat that Oswald supposedly accomplished. Garrison's assistant is shown holding a Mannlicher-Carcano rifle and telling Garrison that the Zapruder film establishes that three shots were fired within 5.6 seconds. The assistant then says, "I'm Oswald, *time me,*" and points the gun out of the window and pretends to shoot three times, squinting through the telescopic scope on the rifle and working the bolt action and pulling the trigger, while Garrison looks at his wrist watch. After the third "shot" Garrison states, "Between 6 and 7 seconds," and the assistant responds, "And that was without really aiming!" The assistant adds, "The key is that the second and third shots came almost on top of each other, but it takes 2.3 seconds to recycle this thing" (i.e., to fire, work the bolt to reload, and fire again). The assistant finally tells Garrison, "Not even the FBI's sharpshooters, no one has ever been able to match Oswald's performance, and he was only a middle grade shot." The assistant finally says, "The scope was even defective." Finally, Garrison concludes, "What they forgot to count on was the Zapruder film; we've got to get it!"

So, could the rifle have been fired *that* fast? The question really has two parts: What was the timing of the actual shots, and how fast can the gun be fired?

Although it is not totally clear what Garrison's assistant in *JFK* meant by "the Zapruder film" showing that all shots were fired within 5.6 seconds, the basic theory seems to have come from the Warren Commission analysis. As noted above, the Warren Commission reviewed a variety of evidence to determine the number and timing of shots, but in the end relied heavily upon the Zapruder film, and the FBI's re-enactment, all of which was based upon various assumptions about what Oswald would and would not have done. Ultimately, the Warren Commission concluded that Oswald had shot three times, that he would not have fired before Zapruder frame 210 (since his view was partially obscured by the oak tree prior to that), that Connally was hit by frame 240, and that the head shot occurred at frame 312. If you accept the assumptions, then the math certainly does reflect that Oswald fired three shots in 5.6 seconds, since $(312-210)/18.3$ frames per second $= 5.6$ seconds. But the resulting conclusion is not purely a math calculation, it is uniquely the result of the underlying assumptions, including the assumption that Oswald would not have fired his first shot until the president has passed out from under the foliage in the live oak tree, as contrasted with other possibilities— such as that he shot through some of the lacy foliage of the tree.

The historical reliance upon questionable assumptions in determining the timing of shots "shown" by the Zapruder film is further illustrated by the Warren Commission's consideration, and rejection, of the possibility that Connally was hit by a *separate* shot (i.e., by a second shot, not the "single bullet") at frames 235–240 (namely, the point at which the Warren Commission believed he first reacted to his wounds). The Warren Commission rejected that possibility since it would mean that the first shot, "assuming a minimum firing time of 2.3 seconds (or 42 frames), was fired between frames 193 and 198 when his view was obscured by the oak tree" and also that "Kennedy continued waving to the crowd after he was hit and did not begin to react for about 1-1/2 seconds [at frames 225–226]." Stated more simply, the Warren Commission rejected the possibility of a shot before frame 210 because (1) it assumed Oswald would have shot after, and not before or through the foliage of the tree, (2) it assumed that Kennedy would have reacted to a hit in less than 1-1/2 seconds, and (3) it assumed—because they did not see any—that there was no reaction by Kennedy before frame 225–226. Of course, if any of those assumptions about human nature and/or what is "visible" in the film are wrong, then a portion of the Warren Commission's rationale for the single bullet theory was wrong, even though (for other, independent reasons) the ultimate "single bullet" conclusion may still be correct. In addition, if any of those assumptions are wrong, the overall timing calculation does not necessarily start with frame 210; it perhaps should start at some earlier point, and the total time span for the three shots could very well be much greater than 5.6 seconds.

Similarly, of course, why do we necessarily assume (simply from the Zapruder film) that the head shot was the last shot—simply because we can see it? In theory (and limiting the evidence to what the Warren Commission had available), Oswald could have fired his last shot after frame 312. If he did, the spacing for three shots is more than 5.6 seconds.

And finally, there is the possibility which even the Warren Commission recognized, that Oswald brought the gun to the Book Depository with an empty casing in it, ejected it on the floor, and only fired *two* shots within 5.6 seconds (or within some other, and perhaps even greater, time span).

In short, the Zapruder film does not prove that Oswald fired three shots within 5.6 seconds. Further, as if that were not quite enough, there is still the second question: How fast can the gun be fired? The Warren Commission was religious in their absolute devotion to the FBI's conclusion that a minimum of 2.3 seconds was required between shots. Their devotion was so great that they often used that number as the benchmark in order to evaluate other available evidence.

Whenever shot timing, and "what the Zapruder film proves" is written about, the conclusions are often wrapped up with the phrase, "Not even the FBI could fire that rifle that fast." Why we should assume that the FBI has the fastest shooters around is an interesting preliminary issue, but trying not to be petty, let's just look at what they did. Did the FBI really fire the rifle as fast as they could fire it?

The truth is that the FBI conducted its test firings upon the basis of *assumptions* about human nature, and specifically assumptions about what Oswald would and would not have been doing and thinking while firing a rifle at the president of the United States. These assumptions have typically gone unstated and uncritically "assumed" to be "fact," even though their validity or lack of validity completely shaped the outcome of their tests.

The FBI conducted its tests using the scope that was mounted on the side of the rifle, and took time to hit the target. Why? Was it because that was what Oswald necessarily would have done. Of course, it may simply have been that the FBI marksmen who tested the rifle did not want to be embarrassed by missing *their* target! But more probably, they were attempting to replicate the actual shooting, and assumed (without really thinking about it) that Oswald would have taken careful aim, careful enough aim to be certain of hitting his target, and assumed that because the rifle had a scope, Oswald would have used it.

For the FBI to have conducted tests to see how quickly the rifle could be shot by taking reasonably careful aim, firing, working the bolt action to load a new shell, taking careful aim, and shooting again, may at first blush even seem to be logical, since the working hypothesis is that Oswald *did* hit his target, and the reason for conducting the tests was to see if that hypothesis is correct. But let me suggest the possibility to you that the assumption that Oswald took careful enough aim to be reasonably sure that he *would* hit his target, is not the *only* reasonable assumption. In fact, that may not even be the *most* reasonable thing to assume.

Imagine how you might feel if you were about to attempt to assassinate the president of the United States. Would some of the emotions running through your mind and driving your adrenaline be excitement, fear, agitation, or (especially if you were slightly crazy) even exhilaration? Would you proceed in a calm, cool and collected manner, doing what might be most rational to accomplish your purpose? Would your actions be dictated more by your mind, or your emotions? Might your first shot be fired even before you were ready, and likewise your second and third?

There is an old expression among deer hunters that describes why so many prize bucks run away unscathed after standing still, broadside in front of a hunter. It's called "buck fever." What produces this "fever" is the excitement of seeing that *biggest of all trophies*, and what often results is firing the gun before it is properly aimed. ("It just went off in my hand.")

The point is that all of the FBI's tests were done with the assumption that the rifle should be carefully aimed before it was fired. If we make the opposite assumption, the time needed to fire, work the bolt to load a new shell, and fire again, is drastically reduced. In fact, I personally took the actual Mannlicher-Carcano rifle that Oswald used—the one that has historically resided in the National Archives—to the Quantico Marine Base in Virginia, and fired it repeatedly with about 1.6 seconds between shots.

And ironically, the assumption that Oswald would have taken the time necessary to be sure he did not miss is actually contrary to the other basic findings of the Warren Commission. Remember, they found that Oswald fired three times, that one shot hit both Kennedy and Connally, and that another shot hit Kennedy. Thus, *Oswald actually missed everything—even the entire limousine—with one of the shots*. How much time is needed to make that kind of "careful" shot!

Furthermore, even if we assume that Oswald did not have "buck fever," and acted cooly, calmly, and rationally, and even if we assume that he fully intended to kill the president and wanted to do the best job he could in completing that task, why would he have used the scope? Let's look at the facts. The rifle was a 6.5 millimeter, Italian made Mannlicher-Carcano, made in 1940. It fired a heavy bullet weighing approximately 160 grains. The scope was an inexpensive, four power scope, stamped "Optics Ordnance Inc./Hollywood California," and "Made in Japan." This was not a fine hunting weapon that fired a flat shooting bullet with great precision. This was not the high-tech assassin's rifle so often portrayed in spy movies, carried to the site broken down into its component parts in a custom made suitcase. (Oswald apparently carried it to work that day in a paper sack.) But Oswald also did not—as the legendary assassin, *Jackal*—set out to shoot someone between the eyes at three hundred yards, either. The distances were short. There was no need to calculate the drop of the bullet for a long shot, or to precisely calculate bullet trajectory based upon the prevailing wind. This was actually a gun that was rather well suited for its intended purpose; a rather crude weapon that shot a heavy bullet quite accurately enough to dependably hit a person at under a hundred yards—even after going through some foliage, if necessary.

The scope was actually somewhat difficult to use, since it was mounted to the side of the rifle. The rifle's standard iron sights, by comparison, were completely exposed (not obstructed by the side-mounted scope) and would have been much easier to use than the scope. Firing time obviously tends to be longer if one takes time to find the target in a scope. When I shot the rifle with 1.6 seconds between shots, I took quick aim using the iron sights, not the scope. And given the fact that this was a moving target at a short distance, iron sights would have been the logical choice. Professional hunters who hunt moving game at close range (particularly, dangerous African game), in fact, usually do not even equip their rifles with scopes because iron sights are more effective.

When the limousine slowed to turn the corner in front of the Book Depository (making a hairpin turn of somewhat more than 90 degrees), it was almost directly below Oswald at a distance of perhaps 40 or 50 yards. It then moved away from him at approximately 11 miles per hour, reaching a maximum distance of perhaps 85 yards when the last of the shots was fired. I have often hunted with a black powder, muzzle loading rifle (like the ones used over a hundred years ago) that shoots a round lead ball, stuffed into the barrel around a cloth patch. Needless to say, it does not have a scope. A shot of less than 100 yards is not particularly difficult. A Mannlicher-Carcano is not a great rifle, but it is as accurate as a muzzle loader.

When we did our acoustic reconstruction, our marksmen used the iron sights, and had no trouble hitting sand bag targets in the street from the sixth floor window of the Book Depository, although, admittedly, the sand bags were not moving. But again, movement of the target only argues more strongly in favor of not using a scope. In short, hitting the limousine's occupants would not have been particularly difficult with iron sights. Locating the target in a scope would have increased the difficulty, and increased the time necessary to fire multiple shots.

At a minimum, even if we assume that Oswald was a lousy shot, he easily could have caused his bullets to hit inside the limousine by just quickly pointing the rifle in that direction and firing. For all we know, that may have been all Oswald really hoped to accomplish: maybe he only wanted to "make a political statement" by spraying the limousine with gun fire, and did not really care if he killed anyone, or if someone were killed, who that someone would be.

My point, of course, is not to suggest that I know what Oswald was really thinking. Rather, I suggest that no one can know what Oswald was thinking. The assumptions that Oswald would not have fired until after frame 210, that he took the time to use the scope, and that he would have aimed carefully, at best, are no more likely to be correct than any number of other possible assumptions. Further, because no one can know what Oswald was thinking, it is clear that the conclusions of the FBI and the Warren Commission both as to the timing of the shots, and the time that Oswald would have taken to fire the rifle, which were based upon such assumptions, cannot be relied upon. And if those conclusions cannot be relied upon, then the conspiracy theories that—ironically—have risen from and been based upon an *acceptance* of the FBI's and Warren Commission's unfounded conclusions, also provide no real answers about what happened.

So, what's the real answer? The basic physical evidence indicates that Oswald fired three shots at the limousine, two of which hit Kennedy and Connally, and thus (as to the question we started with) that Oswald was not a mere patsy. That evidence also indicates that the "single bullet" theory is probably correct. But the Warren Commission's conclusions about the timing of those shots, and their assumptions about how Oswald would have gone about firing them, were merely guesses—probably incorrect guesses—and because those guesses about shot timing are unreliable, all of the intervening conspiracy theories that have been based upon those guesses are also not worthy of belief.

Coincidence, or conspiracy?

One shift in perspective that occurs as the result of conducting a massive investigation like that of the Select Committee, is that the world seems much smaller than it once appeared to be. When massive quantities of data are gathered on the magnitude that they have been in the Kennedy case, you find that everyone is really connected with everyone else. I'm not talking merely about spiritual connection, but connection by concrete events and associations. One of my daughters, Tiffany, loves to play a parlor game called "Sixth Degree," which illustrates the concept. It begins by someone picking a name, usually some famous celebrity, often even in some foreign country, and another player trying to make a connection between himself and the famous celebrity. The connection must be made with no more than six links.

It may sound difficult, but only rarely does it take the full six links to complete the connection. What is the connection between me and Soviet leader Yeltsin? You might be shocked to find out that I have any connection with Yeltsin. Well, I know Bob Blakey, who knows Congressman John Conyers, who knows President Bill Clinton, who knows Yeltsin. Isn't it strange that I have such a close connection with Yeltsin?

One of the early books that questioned the Warren Commission's "no conspiracy" conclusion was called *Coincidence or Conspiracy.* The premise underlying the title was that one or two "coincidental" events may actually be coincidences; but as the "coincidences" pile up, you have to begin to wonder if they are not mere coincidences, and instead have a common cause, in this case, the workings of a conspiracy. Much of the basis for conspiracy theories over the years has followed the logic of that book. Connections—associations—have been found between people or events that appear to be more than coincidence, at least that appear to be more than coincidence when viewed from the perspective of our ordinary lives. Of course, as more and more facts are gathered, more connections are found. In the Kennedy case, the huge scope of investigation over the years, both public and private, has uncovered more and more of such startling connections—and not merely connections "to the sixth degree," but to the first degree—leading to more and more conspiracy possibilities. The problem, of course, is that we may have missed the real lesson to be learned from that extensive investigation: "more coincidences" may not really indicate more conspiracies, but only that the world is much smaller than we realized.

Some additional caution is also required if we are to avoid placing too much reliance upon associations and coincidences, because the Kennedy case is not about the ordinary lives of ordinary people. It is about an extraordinary president who affected large groups of people in extraordinary ways. It is about a chief suspect, Lee Harvey Oswald, whose entire life was a mysterious puzzle of extraordinary associations and activities. It is about extraordinary times, characterized by explosive political and economic tensions and upheaval, and more than ordinary amounts of violence, diverse and overlapping intrigues, and multifarious covert government and underworld activities—times that made many "strange bedfellows." In the early 1960's, America was its usual "melting pot," but it was also more. Trying to solve the case by merely discovering unusual associations and "coincidences" of events would be something akin to discovering an abandoned caldron containing a witch's brew, concluding that the mix of ingredients reveals evil plans, and trying to discern from the potion's smell the identities of both the departed witches and their intended victims.

Because, at least in the context of the Kennedy case, the smell test is an inadequate means to distinguish true coincidences from conspiracy, many conspiracy theories have persisted due simply to a lack of adequate resources to thoroughly investigate the underlying facts. Does the fact that a suspect in the John Kennedy case was staying in the hotel where Bobby Kennedy was killed, on the same night that he was killed, indicate that the two murders may be connected? Is it a coincidence, or evidence of a possible conspiracy? If I told you who the prime John Kennedy suspect was who was staying in the hotel when Bobby Kennedy was killed, what could you do with the information? Could you subpoena the suspect and compel him to testify? What if he took the Fifth Amendment, and refused to say a word on the ground that his testimony might incriminate him? Could you grant him immunity from prosecution and then compel him to testify? What if now (after all of these years) you didn't even know where to find him? What if he had died? Does the hotel still have records that might show if anyone else may have been staying with him? The questions are endless, and the resources necessary to secure answers are seldom available. Over the years, when the resources necessary to separate coincidence from conspiracy have been lacking, the evidentiary gaps, on occasion, have been filled in with speculation.

The Select Committee, as I have said, first tried to decide which conspiracy issues could still be effectively investigated after 15 years, and of those, which were likely to shed significant new light on the major conspiracy theories. Many of those theories were essentially "coincidence-or-conspiracy" issues. Over the following months, many of those conspiracy theories fell apart under closer scrutiny.

One comical example involved the "Umbrella Man." Photographic evidence had earlier revealed that, as the motorcade passed in front of the School Book Depository, an unidentified man pumped an umbrella up and down. It was not raining in Dallas on November 22, 1963, so there was no apparent reason for anyone to even have an umbrella. As he began pumping his umbrella, the shots began. Coincidence, or conspiracy? No one had ever been able to find the man. The photos of him were not clear enough for a good identification. It appeared to some that this might be the key to the entire case, if only the Umbrella Man could be found. But then again, he may have been a victim of the "mysterious deaths" that occurred shortly after the assassination, his critical role in history lost forever. An entire book was written about the possibilities, going so far as to suggest that the umbrella may have been specially rigged to fire some kind of weapon from under its cover.

We took the fuzzy photos and gave them to our panel of photo experts, who enhanced them using computer techniques that were not available to the Warren Commission in 1963. We then published in newspapers across the country the first, ever, clear picture of the Umbrella Man, asking for assistance in identifying him. A call came in to one of our investigators: the Umbrella Man still lived in Dallas! Our investigator arrived at his door, and asked something to the effect, "Do you own an umbrella, and were you in Dealey Plaza on November 22, 1963?" The answer was, "Yes, and please come in."

The Umbrella Man later came to Washington, D.C., brought his umbrella with him, testified in our public hearings, and explained everything. Perhaps the best part of his testimony came when he opened the umbrella to demonstrate to the Committee that it contained no hidden weapons, and it sprang completely inside out, its tines launching outward and scaring the Committee members backwards nearly out of their seats.

He explained that his reason for being in Dealey Plaza with an umbrella was quite obvious. He said that he disliked the Kennedys and—"as everyone knew"—Jack Kennedy's father was a friend of Neville Chamberlain, the British foreign minister during World War II whose policy was to attempt to appease the Nazis. Well, when Chamberlain would appear in public, the British people would protest his foreign policies by pumping their umbrellas up and down, and that's exactly what *he* was doing in Dealey Plaza, protesting Jack Kennedy and *his* policies! As he said, it really was all quite obvious.

There were many such examples where our investigation revealed basic flaws in the conspiracy theories that had arisen over the years from the belief that certain events simply could not be a coincidence. One other example, for illustrative purposes, involved the number of "mysterious deaths" of witnesses and other persons "closely associated" with the case, who had died within a relatively short time after the assassination. Here, the "coincidence-or-conspiracy" analysis led many people to firmly believe there was a conspiracy because of the purported *statistical odds* against "so many people so closely associated with the case" dying "so soon" after the assassination. The deaths included a policeman, a reporter who was closely covering the case, a number of potential witnesses, some associates of people who were close to Jack Ruby and/or Oswald, etc.

We traced the source of this theory to a newspaper article published in the London Times many years earlier, and contacted the newspaper to determine the basis of the statistical calculations. The London Times told us the article had been based upon information provided by a purported statistician whom they quickly discovered to be a charlatan. The story had initially been run in the morning edition but canceled and not run in the afternoon edition. How interesting. The newspaper that reported the story knew within hours that it had no factual basis, but the article continued to provide a rationale for conspiracy theories for years thereafter—and still does!

However, as the investigation progressed, even during the months while our efforts were routinely destroying the historic rationales for almost every conspiracy theory that had been developed over the preceding years—the very theories that had created the political impetus for the formation of the Select Committee in the first place—another thing also began to happen. We gradually began to accumulate more and more small but significant pieces of *new* evidence which suggested the possibility of conspiracy. It was new evidence that did hold up to close scrutiny, evidence of the kind that the Warren Commission said was "beyond the reaches of the government," and yet, evidence that we just kept uncovering.

In some cases, we even concluded that the original theory had validity, even though the basis for the theory was wrong. The "mysterious deaths" was one such case. We found that the original basis for the "mysterious deaths" conspiracy argument was fatally flawed since the "universe" of people from which the "mysterious deaths" had occurred could not be determined, and that was an essential number in order to compute a statistical probability. On the other hand, even though the statistical probability against these deaths occurring could not be mathematically calculated, a number of the deaths *did* involve people who appeared to have truly important information about the case, and they *did* die in very unusual ways, or at suspiciously "coincidental" points in time. One such death was that of Rose Cheramie, who reported to both a lieutenant with the Louisiana State Police and a doctor at the State Hospital in Jackson, Louisiana, on November 20, 1963 that Kennedy was going to be assassinated, then after the assassination reported that she had seen Oswald and Ruby together at Ruby's nightclub in Dallas on numerous occasions. Cheramie was subsequently run over by a speeding car that crushed her skull while she was laying on a highway near Big Sandy, Texas. Her death was ruled by investigating officers to have been an accident (although why she was laying in the road in the first place was never determined).

Another such example was David Ferrie, who the New Orleans coroner said died of natural causes, although two typewritten, unsigned suicide notes were found. During the summer of 1963, Ferrie was working for the Marcello organized crime family, and for militant anti-Castro Cubans headquartered in New Orleans, and for Guy Bannister, the former FBI agent whose office was located in the Newman Building which bore the address 544 Camp Street that was stamped on the pro-Castro literature that Oswald distributed in New Orleans in the summer of 1963. He was also, according to witnesses in Clinton, Louisiana, associated with Oswald. Ferrie died in February, 1967, just after District Attorney Jim Garrison focused his investigation on him. The number, circumstances and timing of such deaths, albeit not the statistical calculations, did suggest the possibility that witnesses had been silenced, and thus, the possibility of conspiracy.

As our investigative efforts proceeded, old theories were destroyed (or came to be viewed in a new light), and at the same time, new evidence of suspicious events continued to emerge. We knew, however, that such evidence only circumstantially suggested the possibility of conspiracy. So we continued to hope that, if we looked long enough and hard enough, if we didn't run out of the congressionally budgeted money and time, and if we got lucky and looked in the right places, we just might find direct evidence of a conspiracy, if it actually existed.

I believe that we were successful.

Was Oswald the only shooter?

There is substantial evidence that Oswald was *not* the only shooter. There were numerous witnesses whom the Warren Commission rejected as not worthy of belief, but whose testimony the Select Committee found was credible, who reported hearing a shot fired from the area of the grassy knoll. One of those witnesses was a railroad supervisor named S. M. Holland, who was standing on the railroad overpass over Elm Street at the time of the assassination. In a sworn deposition taken by the Warren Commission in 1964, Holland said that he heard four shots; that after the first, he saw Governor Connally turn around; that then there was another report; that the first two sounded as if they came from "the upper part of the street;" and that the third was not as loud as the others:

There was a shot, a report. I don't know whether it was a shot. I can't say that. And a puff of smoke came out about 6 or 8 feet above the ground right out from under those trees. And at just about this location from where I was standing, you could see that puff of smoke, like someone had thrown a fire-cracker, or something out, and that is just about the way it sounded. It wasn't as loud as the previous reports or shots.

When counsel for the Warren Commission asked Holland if he had any doubt about the four shots, Holland responded:

I have no doubt about it. I have no doubt about seeing that puff of smoke come out from under those trees either.

Abraham Zapruder, who took his famous film while standing on a concrete abutment near the grassy knoll, also testified in a Warren Commission deposition that he thought a shot may have come from behind him, and he differentiated among the effects the shots had on him, saying that one shot caused reverberations all around him and was much more pronounced than the others.

A secret service agent, Paul Landis, who was riding on the bumper of the follow-up car behind the presidential limousine, wrote a statement on November 30, 1963, in which he described a first shot that "sounded like the report of a high-powered rifle from behind me, over my right shoul-der," and a second shot possibly from a different direction:

I still was not certain from which direction the second shot came, but my reaction at this time was that the shot came from somewhere towards the front, right-hand side of the road.

And an electrician named William Eugene Newman, who was standing with his family near the curb toward the east end of the grassy knoll area, gave a statement on November 22, 1963, in which he said:

> Then we fell down on the grass as it seemed that we were in direct path of fire. . . . I thought the shot had come from the garden directly behind me, that was on an elevation from where I was as I was right on the curb. I do not recall looking toward the Texas School Book Depository. I looked back in the vicinity of the garden.

The photographic evidence corroborates Newman's testimony, showing him doing exactly what he described in his statement.

The Warren Commission perhaps rejected such testimony because they found no physical corroboration for it. But the Select Committee did develop scientific evidence that corroborated the testimony of those witnesses. That evidence strongly indicates that two shooters fired at the presidential limousine as it passed through Dealey Plaza.

The Committee discovered tape recordings containing the Dallas Police Department dispatch radio transmissions made over both Channel I and Channel II of the police radio network on the day of the assassination. The recordings on Channel I appeared to contain transmissions that came from a motorcycle with a stuck microphone that was passing through Dealey Plaza at the exact time the fatal shots were fired. The microphones on the police motorcycles frequently became stuck, since they were surrounded by a rubber grommet that often became hard and brittle from the weather, and when the button was depressed it simply remained in the "on" position for some time. The Channel I transmissions, which had been recorded on a Dictabelt recorder in the police station as they were received, appeared to contain approximately 5 minutes of such constant transmissions from a stuck microphone. We gave the tapes to Bolt, Beranek and Newman, located in Cambridge, Massachusetts, for further analysis.

The scientists at Bolt, Beranek and Newman are among the nation's top experts in acoustical analysis, the science of analyzing the nature and origin of sound impulses. They had been instrumental in designing much of the Navy's underwater sonar equipment used to locate enemy submarines, and had pioneered the use of sound recordings to pinpoint the location of gunfire from recorded sounds in connection with the Kent State shootings, where students were shot by National Guardsmen in 1970. Bolt, Beranek had also been chosen by Judge Sirica to serve on the panel that examined the Watergate tapes in 1973. Bolt, Beranek's analysis of the Dallas Police Department tapes was personally supervised by their chief scientist, Dr. James Barger.

The basic scientific principles that allow the origin of a loud, impulsive sound to be determined from a recording made by a single microphone have been known for over a hundred years, but they had never been applied in a context like this before Bolt, Beranek did it at Kent State in 1970. There is no evidence that the Warren Commission considered using this type of analysis (although they did analyze other tape recordings for other purposes in 1964).

The preliminary analysis by Bolt, Beranek reflected that the Channel I recording contained six separate groups of impulses (each group containing its own unique sequence or pattern of impulses) that might be recorded gunshots, all of which:

- Occurred during the period of the assassination;
- Were unique to the time period of the assassination (i.e., did not occur elsewhere on the tape);
- In total time (from first to last) lasted long enough to roughly correspond to the approximate duration of the assassination as indicated by photographic evidence (with the realization that independent evidence did not establish this total time with any real precision);
- Had impulse pattern shapes that resembled the shape of impulse patterns produced when the sound of gunfire is recorded through a radio transmission system comparable to the one used for the Dallas police dispatch network; and
- Had impulse pattern amplitudes similar to those produced when the sound of gunfire is recorded through a radio transmission system comparable to the one used for the Dallas police dispatch network.

Upon the basis of their preliminary examination, Bolt, Beranek advised that further testing was merited.

The ability to pinpoint the origin or location of an impulsive sound like a gun shot solely from a sound recording derives from the fact that when such a loud sound occurs, it travels outward in all directions at a constant rate of speed (the speed is affected slightly by temperature and humidity, which of course could be determined from weather records for November 22, 1963), bounces off of the nearby echo-producing structures (which in a complex urban environment like Dealey Plaza are all "randomly spaced"), and then continues onward at the same rate of speed until it finally dissipates. If a recording is made of the sound of the gun shot and the resulting echoes, the recorded sound impulses can be visually displayed on an oscilloscope or oscillograph (electronic instruments which display sound as visual wave patterns). Because the speed of the sound is constant, the only variable is distance, and thus the first sound to arrive at the microphone—and the first blip or spike on the oscillograph—will be the sound that traveled the shortest distance, namely, the sound of the actual gun shot, since it traveled in a straight line from the gun to the microphone. (As we know, the shortest distance between two points is a straight line.) The next sound impulse recorded will be the sound of the echo produced by the echo-producing source that was closest to the straight line path from the rifle to the microphone (i.e., the sound that traveled the second shortest distance), and so on. If the sound of a gunshot together with its significant echos were to last one second, you could conceptualize the oscillograph printout as a string of 1,000 little boxes (i.e., dividing the full second into milliseconds). If there were six significant echos recorded, the original gunshot sound would fill box #1. The first significant echo might be in box #236 (having arrived 236 milliseconds later), the next in box 278, the next in box 303, the next in box 329, the next in box 452 and the last in box 525.

Now, of course, if you move either the shooter location, or the microphone location, all of the echo travel distances would change and six different boxes would be filled. What are the odds against merely accidentally (or randomly) filling any given set of boxes? Perhaps not quite as high as the odds against throwing a hand full of loose watch parts up into the air and having them fall into an assembled watch on the floor, but they are very high. Any given set of boxes is a unique "pattern," the same sort of *random pattern* as a fingerprint, or a tire print in the mud (showing randomly spaced cuts, punctures, and uneven tire wear)—the kind of random pattern upon which people are often convicted and sent to jail, since it is typically viewed as proof "beyond a reasonable doubt."

Thus, we felt that *if* we could go to Dealey Plaza and create new sound patterns that *matched* those on the Dallas Police tape (i.e., that contained echos that filled the same "boxes") by shooting live ammunition from different locations at targets that were approximately in the same location as the limousine, and recording the sounds at the same locations as the supposed motorcycle had been located when its radio transmitted the original sounds, we would know exactly where the shots had been fired that created the original police department impulse patterns on November 22, 1963.

On August 20, 1978, we went to Dealey Plaza. The Police Department sealed off the Plaza (although news camera crews from stations all over the world watched from all of the adjoining roof tops). We placed sand bags at the approximate locations where we believed bullets may have struck, we positioned twelve microphones spaced 18 feet apart down the middle of the street (starting on Houston Street), and police marksmen fired live ammunition into the sand bags while we recorded the sounds. A Mannlicher-Carcano rifle was fired from the sixth floor Book Depository window. Both a Mannlicher-Carcano rifle and a pistol (because it fired a subsonic bullet) were fired from behind the fence on the grassy knoll. After recording the sounds from the first 12 microphones, they were moved to cover the next section of the street, and the tests shots were repeated. In the end, we had recorded 432 "test patterns" that were then taken back to the lab to see if any of them matched the sounds on the original Channel I Dictabelt.

After the initial comparison of the test patterns with the original tape, Bolt, Beranek determined that there was a 99% statistical probability that the Channel I recordings contained impulse patterns from gun shots, and that it appeared that three shots had come from the Book Depository, and one from the grassy knoll.

However, because we had limited time to seal off

Dealey Plaza and fire live ammunition, we had to limit the number of "test patterns" that we could obtain. The limitation was achieved by spacing the microphones 18 feet apart, and placing them in the middle of the street. It was thus unlikely that any microphone was located precisely where the original motorcycle was located when the shots were fired. To deal with the resulting imprecision in microphone location, and thus, the imprecision in data that would appear in the test patterns, test echos were considered to "match" original DPD tape echos if they were within $+/-$ 6/1000 of a second. Nevertheless, even with that built in ambiguity, Bolt, Beranek determined that there was an 88% statistical probability that match one was a shot from the Book Depository, an 88% statistical probability that match two was a shot from the Book Depository, a 50% statistical probability that match three was a shot from the grassy knoll, and a 75% statistical probability that match four was a shot from the Book Depository.

Because the Committee's term was running out, and because the other physical evidence strongly corroborated the acoustical findings as to the three shots from the Book Depository, the Committee decided to focus the remaining efforts primarily on the acoustical evidence about a possible shot from the grassy knoll. In mid-September, 1978, the Committee asked Professor Mark Weiss of Queens College of the City University of New York (who had served on the Watergate tape panel in 1973, and was recommended to the Committee by the Acoustical Society of America) to work with Bolt, Beranek to try to refine the data, particularly focusing on the possible shot from the grassy knoll.

By now, what were believed upon the basis of "acoustics theory" to be the principal echo-producing sources in Dealey Plaza, had been confirmed through the testing, and the actual travel patterns of each echo for the grassy knoll shot was known. More particularly, the exact travel time (and the exact travel distance) for each such echo was known. In their lab, Professor Weiss and his assistant, Ernie Aschkenasy, thus began to move the shooter location that we had arbitrarily chosen for our test shots, down the picket fence a few feet at a time, and move the microphone location (where the grassy knoll shot had been recorded in our tests) gradually away from its position in the middle of the street, readjusting the echos for each new location, and looking for a combination of shooter location and microphone location that would make all of the echos match.

The match with this more precise technique did not have to be only within $+/-6/1,000$ of a second, but now was possible within $1/1,000$ of a second. Near the end of this process, they got close, but could not get all of the echos to match with any single combination of shooter and microphone location until they realized that the motorcycle would have been moving during the time that the echos were recorded. With a microphone location near the curb (instead of in the middle of the street as it had been during the test firings) and by adjusting for its movement (at 11 mph), and with the shooter location moved to the west of the test location and onto the main part of the fence that ran parallel to the street, the echoes matched. Bolt, Beranek agreed with Weiss and Aschkenasy that their refinement of the data now indicated that a shot had been fired from the grassy knoll to a 95% statistical probability.

But it wasn't just a matter of statistical probability. First, the locations of the microphones that recorded the four separate matching test patterns (three from the Book Depository, and one from the grassy knoll) were known, and thus the distances between those microphones were also known. In addition, of course, the time spacing of the sound patterns on the original Dictabelt tape was known. If you know time and distance, you can calculate speed, and the calculation reflected that the four microphones that recorded the matching test patterns were "traveling down the street" at the same speed (approximately 11 mph) as the motorcade had been traveling on November 22, 1963.

Further, when a supersonic bullet goes through the air, it makes a wake (a shock wave), much the same as the wake that a boat makes in the water. That shock wave travels outward in a direct path that resembles a cone (as contrasted with the muzzle blast, which travels outward in all directions, spreading spherically). The shock wave would also be recorded by a microphone, provided the microphone was in its line of travel, and not behind it. The shock wave would only hit a microphone located within the area lying in front of the shooter, within approximately 45 degrees on either side of the path of the bullet. For the shots that would have been aimed in such a direction that the motorcycle's microphone should have picked up the shock wave, including shot #3 from the grassy knoll, the DPD recording showed the shockwave.

The testing also revealed that the plastic windshield on the DPD motorcycles somewhat distorted the sound impulses received by the radio. The tests indicated that the motorcycle was traveling approximately 120 feet behind the presidential limousine. So for shots one and two from the Book Depository, and shot three from the grassy knoll, the motorcycle windshield would have been between the shooter and the microphone. As expected, for those shots the DPD dispatch tape reflected the distortions from the windshield. For shot four, when the microphone was between the shooter in the Book Depository and the windshield, there was no distortion in the sound pattern on the original DPD recording.

Finally, the testing reflected that the recorded sounds on the DPD tape were too loud to have been something like a typical firecracker, and because they were shown to have originated very precisely from the picket fence on the grassy knoll, they could not have been something like the backfire of a motorcycle. And when we reviewed the photographic evidence in light of the acoustical findings, we found that indeed a motorcycle was traveling in the location that had been indicated by the acoustical tests.

If the results of the acoustical tests can be believed, which I certainly think they can, then the timing of the shots was as follows:

Shot # (and Origin)	Time of Day (DPD tape time)	Zapruder Frames	Elapsed Time Since Previous Shot	Total Elapsed Time Since 1st Shot	Comments
1st (From TSBD)	12:30:47.0	157–161			
		166			WC: Limo passed under foliage of oak tree, obstructing view of president
2nd (From TSBD)	12:30:48.6	188–191	1.6	1.6	WC: brief view of Kennedy through oak tree at frame 186
		200			SCA: 1st point at which Kennedy can be seen reacting to wounds
		200–206			View of Connally becomes obscured by sign
		205–225			Kennedy behind sign (cannot be seen in Z film)
		210			WC: Kennedy clearly visible after limo passes beyond oak tree
		222–226			SCA: 1st point at which Connally can be seen reacting to wounds (as he emerges from behind sign)
3rd (Grassy Knoll)	12:30:54.6	295–296	6	7.6	SCA forensic pathology panel (with one dissenting vote): this shot missed.
4th (From TSBD)	12:30:55.3	312	.7	8.3	Frame in which shot to Kennedy's head can be seen

In reviewing the information set forth above, it should be kept in mind that the Warren Commission (in typical Warren Commission fashion) somewhat overstated the precision of its re-enactment data, including its conclusions about whether visibility from the sixth floor window was obstructed by the oak tree at certain Zapruder frames. In the course of writing this book, I found a memo from one of the Select Committee's photo experts, William K. Hartman, senior scientist for the Planetary Science Institute in Tucson, Arizona, addressed to Committee staff members Michael Goldsmith and Jane Downey, on February 5, 1979, discussing this issue and giving a more accurate description of the interference from the oak tree:

> Much has been made of the limitations placed by the FBI on possible firing times, based on their determination of when the President was obstructed by the tree, as seen from the 6th floor window, TSBD. On May 24, 1964, they determined JFK passed "into foliage" in frame 166 (WCE 889), appeared in an opening in frame 186 (WCE 891), and emerged at frame 210 (WCE 893). *The exhibits themselves indicate that the car can be easily tracked through the foliage at many points between 166 and 210,* so that 166 and 210 are conservative, wide limits.

As viewed from the sixth floor window, the limousine did not pass behind the oak tree's trunk, but rather along and through the outer perimeter of its foliage. Because that foliage was not a solid mass, the limousine could be seen moving through it (and a heavy bullet like the Mannlicher-Carcano could have been fired through it)—obviously, at some points more easily than at others. When and to what degree sight was obstructed was, therefore, necessarily a matter of approximation and of relativity. The "view" was simply better at some times than at others: it was not cut off precisely at frame 166; the next clear view was not precisely limited to frame 186 (but rather covered perhaps 2 or 3 or 4 frames around 186), etc.

The findings of Bolt, Beranek and Newman—like almost everything in the Kennedy case—have subsequently been questioned by the FBI, and by a panel assembled by the National Research Council (whose members are drawn from the Councils of the National Academy of Sciences, a congressionally chartered, private, nonprofit agency that provides "services to the government, the public, and the scientific and engineering communities"). According to a "Notice" on the first page of the NRC report, the committee that studied the BBN findings "was chosen for their special competence and with regard for appropriate balance"—not because they were acoustics experts, which they were not.

I personally found it interesting not only that the NRC found that it had conclusively disproved the Select Committee's acoustical report and that there was no need for further study, but also that—remarkably, and just as with the findings of the Warren Commission—there was not a single dissent among any of the panel's members. (It may or may not also be relevant that, among the most vocal of the panel's members was a scientist who, before joining the panel and reviewing the acoustical study in detail, had taken strong positions in support of the Warren Commission's findings that there was no conspiracy. I recognize that may be irrelevant, since he certainly may have put aside any preconceptions he formed from his earlier work, and his assistance to the NRC may have been conducted without any bias stemming from his prior position on the issue.)

The NRC's principal rationale for rejecting the findings of Bolt, Beranek and Mark Weiss was that the Channel I tape contained "cross-talk" from Channel II that indicated that the portion of the Channel I tape containing the four impulse patterns identified as gun fire occurred at least 30 seconds after the actual assassination. The NRC offered possible (plausible) explanations as to various ways that such cross-talk could have gotten onto Channel I, including that the stuck microphone on Channel I was positioned near another microphone that was monitoring Channel II, and that the words being transmitted over Channel II were picked up (very faintly) by the stuck Channel I microphone, and transmitted and recorded on the Channel I Dictabelt in the police station. Subsequent re-recording is another possible explanation. The NRC in the end was not able to definitively state the cause. Nor were they able to verify that the Channel I tape they analyzed was the original DPD tape, and thus could not say for sure that the cross-talk had been recorded on November 22, 1963. Finally, subsequent private analysis as well as further review by Dr. Barger has revealed that the NRC's tests appear to have been conducted with the tapes being run at an improper speed, thus invalidating their calculations of when the impulse patterns at issue actually did occur in relation to the assassination.

And the NRC essentially ignored, and never did explain how, if these impulse patterns were not gun fire, their timing, sequencing, and qualitative characteristics were so extensively corroborated by the other physical and scientific evidence in the case. Was all of the meshing of such evidence simply a coincidence? The acoustics indicated three shots from the Book Depository, where the rifle and shell casings were found. Just a coincidence? The acoustics indicated that sounds were recorded by a motorcycle located in a particular place at particular times, and photographic evidence confirmed that there was a motorcycle exactly where the acoustics indicated it would be. Just a coincidence? The acoustics indicated not only that the microphone was moving but that it was traveling at 11 MPH, just the speed of the actual motorcade. More coincidence? Several witnesses testified that one shot came from the grassy knoll, just as the acoustics indicated. Just a coincidence? The shock waves and windshield distortions were present on the shots where they should have been, and absent on the others. One more coincidence? Since the NRC described their findings as conclusive and not subject to question, one must wonder why the NRC ignored all of this evidence that corroborated the Barger and Weiss findings, but is totally inconsistent with the NRC finding that these impulses are not the actual sounds of gunfire. One might also wonder why the NRC never addressed, never discussed, and never attempted to explain other "cross talk" on the Channel I tape that is totally incon-sistent with the NCR conclusion that the impulse patterns ev-idencing four shots occurred 30 seconds after the actual the assassination.

The NRC admitted that further study was possible, and they as well as Bolt, Beranek suggested a number of things that could be done to resolve the issues raised by the NRC study, but the NRC offered the opinion that further study would not be worth the expense. Isn't that a political question, whether it is worth the expense? Why was the NRC offering political opinions, instead of sticking to the sci-entific issue of whether further study might lead to more definitive conclusions?

If there were, in fact, two shooters (as I believe the best available data indicates), then there was a conspiracy. I say that because the only other possibility would be that two independent shooters coincidentally attempted to kill the president of the United States at the same moment in time, and fired from only a few hundred feet apart, without either of them having known in advance that the other would be present carrying out similar intentions or without some third person or group having put the two of them up to it. Yes, that's right, even in the Kennedy case some "coincidences" are sufficient, without more, to support the conclusion that there was a conspiracy.

The Scene of the Crime

(Aerial view of Dealey Plaza, Dallas, Texas. Arrows show approximate locations of shooters indicated by physical and eyewitness evidence and acoustics testing.)

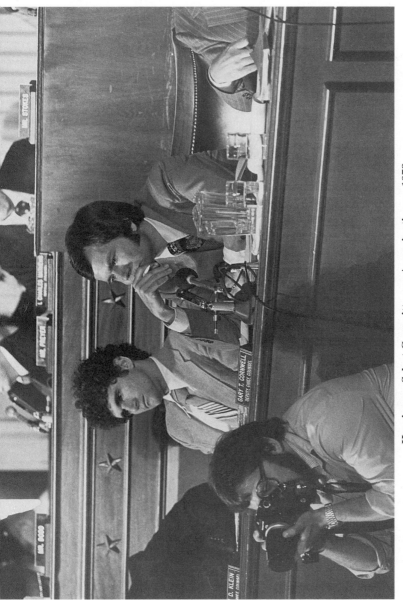

Hearings—Select Committee on Assassinations—1978

(On right, author Gary Cornwell, Deputy Chief Counsel; on left, Kenneth D. Klein, Assistant Deputy Chief Counsel.)

President Gerald R. Ford

(Former President Ford, providing testimony about his service on the Warren Commission in 1963–64.
Select Committee hearings, September 21, 1978.)

"The Umbrella Man"

(Louie Steven Witt, testifying before the Select Committee, September 25, 1978.)

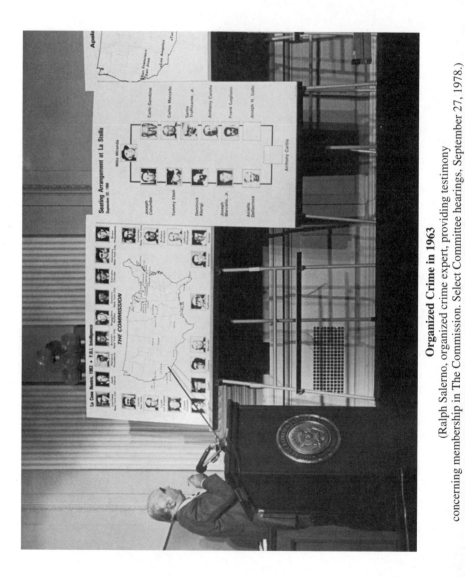

Organized Crime in 1963

(Ralph Salerno, organized crime expert, providing testimony concerning membership in The Commission. Select Committee hearings, September 27, 1978.)

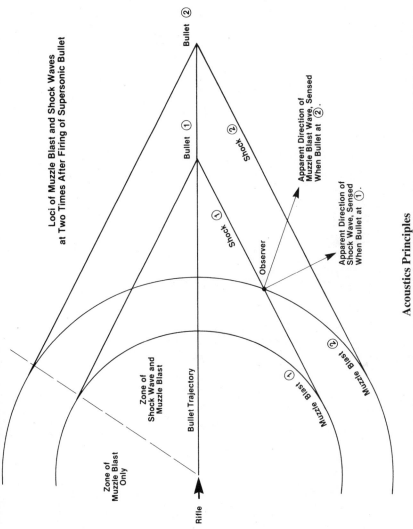

**Loci of Muzzle Blast and Shock Waves
at Two Times After Firing of Supersonic Bullet**

Bullet ②

Bullet ①

Shock ②

Shock ①

Apparent Direction of
Muzzle Blast Wave, Sensed
When Bullet at ②.

Apparent Direction of
Shock Wave, Sensed
When Bullet at ①.

Observer

Muzzle Blast ②

Muzzle Blast ①

Zone of
Shock Wave and
Muzzle Blast

Zone of
Muzzle Blast
Only

Bullet Trajectory

Rifle

Acoustics Principles

(Diagram illustrating spread of shock wave and muzzle blast. Select Committee Exhibit F-357.)

Acoustics Tests

(Photo looking west on Elm Street, showing microphones and sand bag targets during acoustics tests: August 20, 1978.)

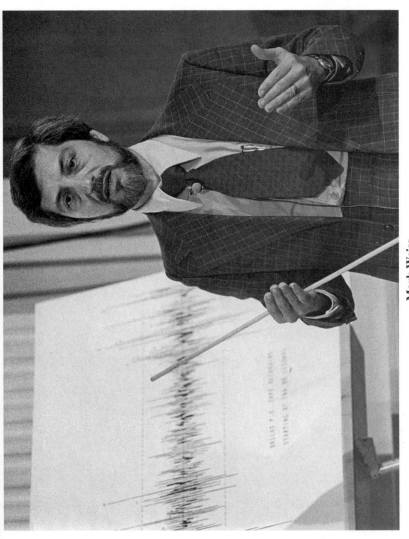

Mark Weiss

(Acoustics expert, Professor Mark Weiss, Queens College, City University of New York, testifying concerning shot from the grassy knoll, December 29, 1978.)

FRAME 186

PHOTOGRAPH FROM RE-ENACTMENT

PHOTOGRAPH FROM ZAPRUDER FILM

PHOTOGRAPH THROUGH RIFLE SCOPE

DISTANCE TO STATION C .... 116.3 FT.

DISTANCE TO RIFLE IN WINDOW ...... 156.3 FT.

ANGLE TO RIFLE IN WINDOW .... 24°03'

DISTANCE TO OVERPASS .... 371.7 FT.

ANGLE TO OVERPASS .... 0°03'

Warren Commission Shot Reenactment —May 24, 1964

(Warren Commission Exhibit 891 showing approximate view from 6th floor window at Zapruder film frame number 186.)

The Oak Tree

(Photo taken by Secret Service from 6th floor of TSBD, December 5, 1963, showing limousine passing through edges of oak tree foliage. WC Exhibit 875.)

If there was a conspiracy,
who was involved in it?

There are two basic approaches to identifying the other conspirators. The difference between the approaches is essentially like looking through the opposite ends of a funnel. You can start with Oswald, and his known history and known associates (both those who have previously been identified and those who have not), and look for suspects. Like looking through the small end of the funnel, in Oswald's case (given his bizarre history of travels and seemingly contradictory associations) this approach leads to an ever expanding universe of possible suspects. Or, you can begin with the traditional question of who had the motive, opportunity, and means to commit the crime. That approach is like looking through the wide mouth of the funnel, beginning with the suspects—the Mafia, Russia, Cuba, right-wing southern extremists, the anti-Castro Cubans, the military-industrial complex, etc.—and attempting to narrow the possibilities by determining whether those persons or groups who had the motive also were in contact with Oswald. The Select Committee employed both approaches, and in the process uncovered and confirmed the validity of volumes of intriguing evidence. The problem was, as I briefly noted earlier, that after fifteen years only some of the necessary investigative techniques that typically produce definitive or at least highly probable solutions to crimes were still viable, and even those techniques had their limitations.

To take an example, on April 10, 1963, about two weeks prior to his move from Dallas to New Orleans, Oswald apparently attempted to kill Major General Edwin A. Walker. Walker had resigned from the U.S. Army in 1961, and was a publicly active right-wing conservative who was widely recognized in Dallas for his anti-communism views. Upon the basis of the physical evidence, Marina Oswald's testimony, and a handwritten note left by Oswald on the evening of the shooting giving instructions to Marina as to the location of the jail and what she should do if he was "taken prisoner," the Warren Commission concluded that Oswald fired the bullet which entered through a window of Walker's home, narrowly missed Walker's head while he was seated at his desk, then went through a wall, and came to rest in the adjoining room.

Because critics had challenged the Warren Commission's conclusion that Oswald was involved, the Select Committee's handwriting experts analyzed the note that Oswald left for Marina, and our firearms and neutron activation experts analyzed the bullet which had been recovered from the house. Although the bullet was too mutilated to positively determine that it came from Oswald's rifle, all of the data indicated that it was probably a Mannlicher-Carcano bullet. Taken together, the available science confirmed the Warren Commission's conclusion that Oswald was involved.

But the most interesting information was that Oswald may not have acted alone. There were no eyewitnesses to the shooting, but a friend of Walker's reported seeing two men two nights before the shooting, snooping around the house and peeking into windows. Another witness reported seeing two men driving away from a church parking lot next to the Walker's home immediately after the shooting. If Oswald did have an accomplice in his attempt to shoot Walker only six months prior to his attempt on Kennedy, the importance of identifying such an accomplice is obvious. But the Select Committee had no scientific method, or other means to effectively pursue this potentially significant information fifteen years after the event.

For similar reasons, the Committee investigated Oswald's political activities (including his contacts with both pro-Castro and anti-Castro activists) in New Orleans in the summer of 1963, and identified and interviewed many of the persons he was involved with there. However, we could not identify or locate all of those associates, or reach definitive conclusions about whether they were in contact with

118

him a few months later, at the time of the assassination in November.

During the 1964 investigation the FBI received information that Oswald was in the company of two anti-Castro Cubans in September 1963, and that they visited a woman named Silvia Odio, who was a member of the anti-Castro organization known as JURE. In testimony before the Warren Commission, Mrs. Odio said that in late September (probably, September 26 or 27, but certainly before October 1) three men came to her home in Dallas to ask for help in preparing a fund-raising letter for JURE. She said that two of the men, who appeared to be Cubans although they also had characteristics that she associated with Mexicans, used the war names "Leopoldo" and "Angelo." The third man, an American, was introduced as "Leon Oswald."

Mrs. Odio said that the three men told her they had just come from New Orleans, and that they were about to leave on a trip. The next day, one of the Cubans (or Mexicans) called her on the telephone and told her that it had been his idea to introduce the American into the underground "because he is great, he is kind of nuts." He also told her that the American had been in the Marine Corps and was an excellent shot, and that the American had said that Cubans "don't have any guts . . . because President Kennedy should have been assassinated after the Bay of Pigs, and some Cubans should have done that, because he was the one that was holding the freedom of Cuba actually." Both Mrs. Odio and her sister identified the American as Lee Harvey Oswald.

The Warren Commission rejected the Odio testimony—in large part upon the basis of purported evidence that Oswald was on a bus on his way to Mexico on the date of the alleged visit—even though at the time its final Report went to press, the Warren Commission knew that the FBI had not completed its investigation of Odio's story. Furthermore, the purported "bus to Mexico" evidence was described in an internal memo by Warren Commission staff attorney J. Wesley Liebler, as really being "no evidence at all."

The Committee attempted to verify the story, and locate the unknown companions, "Leopoldo" and "Angelo." Dr. Burton Einspruch, Mrs. Odio's doctor, confirmed that Mrs. Odio had told him about the visit shortly after it occurred, but prior to the president's assassination. From FBI files, the Committee secured a list of persons who belonged to the Dallas Chapter of JURE, and attempted to locate and interview them. We located and interviewed Manolo Ray, the leader of JURE who was then living in Puerto Rico. We secured photos of scores of pro-Castro and anti-Castro activists who fit the descriptions given by Mrs. Odio. We asked the CIA to try to identify individuals who used the war names Leopoldo and Angelo, and the CIA produced three photos of men who might have been in Dallas in September 1963. Mrs. Odio was not able to identify any of the photos as being "Leopoldo" or "Angelo" after all of the intervening years. In the end, the Committee believed Mrs. Odio's story, and rejected the Warren Commission's conclusion that Oswald could not have been in Dallas when the visit occurred, but was not able to identify the apparent Cuban associates of Oswald.

The Committee also investigated Oswald's trip to Mexico City in September 1963, when he visited the Cuban Consulate, apparently visited the campus of the National Autonomous University of Mexico, and "with two companions" (according to the testimony of Mexican author Elena Garro de Paz) attended a "twist party" at the home of Ruben Duran, brother-in-law of Silvia Duran, the secretary of Cuban consul Eusebio Azcue. In the end, potentially important associates of Oswald could not be identified after fifteen years, and the true significance of Oswald's trip to Mexico City could not be determined. As to those as well as many other allegations relating to the broader issue of a possible Cuban conspiracy, the Committee reluctantly concluded that

> . . . a definitive answer had to come, if at all, largely from the investigation conducted in 1963–64 by the Warren Commission and the FBI and CIA. What the committee was able to do 15 years later could fill in important details, but it could not make up for basic insufficiencies. Unfortunately, the committee found that there were in fact significant deficiencies in the earlier investigation . The Warren Commission knew far less than it professed to know about Oswald's trip to Mexico and his possible association with pro-Castro agents in Mexico and elsewhere. This was true, in part, because the Commission had demanded less of the FBI and CIA than called for in its mandate.

The result of the Committee's attempts to determine who may have been involved with Oswald in a conspiracy

121

was a number of intriguing possible answers—some conflicting, some overlapping. There was more and better evidence in some areas than in others, with perhaps the best evidence relating to the organized crime and Cuban activists groups with whom both Oswald and Ruby had contacts. But it may not be that an organized crime and/or Cuban conspiracy is really the most "probable" answer. Instead, it may simply be that it was in those areas that the Committee was able to find the most evidence.

The existence of the second shooter, as indicated by the acoustics evidence which was developed near the end of the Committee's investigation, raises its own host of interesting issues, and it produced at least in theory the possibility for *narrowing* the list of suspects. If there were two shooters, then the second shooter and/or associates of the second shooter would necessarily also have been an associate—or associates of an associate—of Oswald. The quandary, of course, is how, at this late date, to move beyond mere evidence of the existence of a second shooter, and determine his (or her) identity.

*What was the most significant
finding of the Select Committee
on Assassinations?*

Most people are surprised when I tell them what the findings of the Select Committee were—especially that the Committee concluded that there was a conspiracy—and that those findings were made public. Actually, the Committee's final Report, which was 261 pages long, plus twelve backup volumes of hearing transcripts and staff reports totaling several thousand pages more, was printed in its entirety in 1979 by the Government Printing Office (GPO), and it can be found in major libraries throughout the United States.

Part of the lack of knowledge is due to the fact that the only private printing to date has been a 1979 paperback edition by Bantam Books (of the basic report, without supporting volumes). The Bantam edition of the Report, which was styled *The Final Assassinations Report,* has long been out of print, although it can still occasionally be found in used book stores.

The main findings of the Select Committee, as summarized in the Table of Contents to the final Report, were that:

- Lee Harvey Oswald fired three shots at President John F. Kennedy. The second and third shots he fired struck the president. The third shot he fired killed the president.
  - President Kennedy was struck by two rifle shots fired from behind him.
  - The shots that struck President Kennedy from behind him were fired from the sixth floor window of the southeast corner of the Texas School Book Depository building.
  - Lee Harvey Oswald owned the rifle that was used to fire the shots from the sixth floor window of the southeast corner of the Texas School Book Depository building.
  - Lee Harvey Oswald, shortly before the assassination, had access to and was present on the sixth floor of the Texas School Book Depository building.
  - Lee Harvey Oswald's other actions tend to support the conclusion that he assassinated President Kennedy.

- Scientific acoustical evidence establishes a high probability that two gunmen fired at President John F. Kennedy.
- Other scientific evidence does not preclude the possibility of two gunmen firing at the president.
- Scientific evidence negates some specific conspiracy allegations.
- The committee believes, on the basis of the available evidence, that President John F. Kennedy was probably assassinated as a result of a conspiracy.
- The committee is unable to identify the other gunman or the extent of the conspiracy.
- The committee believes, on the basis of the available evidence, that:
  - the Soviet Government was not involved in the assassination of President Kennedy;
  - the Cuban Government was not involved in the assassination of President Kennedy;
  - anti-Castro Cuban groups, *as groups,* were not involved in the assassination of President Kennedy, but that the available evidence does not preclude the possibility that individual members may have been involved;
  - the national syndicate of organized crime, *as a group,* was not involved in the assassination of President Kennedy, but that the available evidence does not preclude the possibility that individual members may have been involved;

- the Secret Service, Federal Bureau of Investigation and Central Intelligence Agency were not involved in the assassination of President Kennedy.
- Agencies and departments of the U.S. Government performed with varying degrees of competency in the fulfillment of their duties. President John F. Kennedy did not receive adequate protection. A thorough and reliable investigation into the responsibility of Lee Harvey Oswald for the assassination of President John F. Kennedy was conducted. The investigation into the possibility of conspiracy in the assassination was inadequate. The conclusions of the investigations were arrived at in good faith, but presented in a fashion that was too definitive.
- The Secret Service was deficient in the performance of its duties.
  - The Secret Service possessed information that was not properly analyzed, investigated or used by the Secret Service in connection with the president's trip to Dallas; in addition, Secret Service agents in the motorcade were inadequately prepared to protect the president from a sniper.
  - The responsibility of the Secret Service to investigate the assassination was terminated when the Federal Bureau of Investigation assumed primary investigative responsibility.
- The Department of Justice failed to exercise initiative in supervising and directing the investigation

by the Federal Bureau of Investigation of the assassination.

- The Federal Bureau of Investigation (FBI) performed with varying degrees of competency in the fulfillment of its duties.
  - The FBI adequately investigated Lee Harvey Oswald prior to the assassination and properly evaluated the evidence it possessed to assess his potential to endanger the public safety in a national emergency.
  - The FBI conducted a thorough and professional investigation into the responsibility of Lee Harvey Oswald for the assassination.
  - The FBI failed to investigate adequately the possibility of a conspiracy to assassinate the president.
  - The FBI was deficient in its sharing of information with other agencies and departments.
- The Central Intelligence Agency (CIA) was deficient in its collection and sharing of information both prior to and subsequent to the assassination.
- The Warren Commission performed with varying degrees of competency in the fulfillment of its duties.
  - The Warren Commission conducted a thorough and professional investigation into the responsibility of Lee Harvey Oswald for the assassination.
  - The Warren Commission failed to investigate adequately the possibility of a conspiracy to assassi-

nate the president. This deficiency was attributable in part to the failure of the Commission to receive all the relevant information that was in the possession of other agencies and departments of the Government.

- The Warren Commission arrived at its conclusions, based on the evidence available to it, in good faith.
- The Warren Commission presented the conclusions in its report in a fashion that was too definitive.

The most important of those findings, at least in my opinion, is not set out as one of the principal findings above. It appears as a subcategory to the last principal finding in the Report. It is the finding which, I would submit, was based upon the greatest degree of certainty—about which there is the least room for doubt. It is a finding with which I not only agree, but which I am convinced is accurate to a moral certainty.

When their president was killed in 1963, what the American public most wanted to know—and had a right to be told, if possible—was, *Who was responsible* for their president's death? The Warren Commission's *principal responsibility* was to answer that question. As stated in the Foreword to the Warren Commission's Final Report:

President Lyndon B. Johnson, by Executive Order No. 11130 dated November 29, 1963, created this Commission to investigate the assassination on November 22, 1963, of John Fitzgerald Kennedy, the 35th President of the United States. The President directed the Commission to evaluate **all the facts and circumstances surrounding the assassination and the subsequent killing of the alleged assassin [Lee Harvey Oswald]** and to report its findings and conclusions to him.

※　　※　　※

Alternative means for instituting a **complete investigation** were widely discussed. Federal and State officials conferred on the possibility of initiating a court of inquiry before a State magistrate in Texas. An investigation by the grand jury of Dallas County also was considered. As speculation about the existence of a foreign or domestic conspiracy became widespread, committees in both Houses of Congress weighed the desirability of congressional hearings to discover all the facts relating to the assassination.

※　　※　　※

By his order of November 29 establishing the Commission, President Johnson sought to avoid parallel investigations and to concentrate fact finding in a body having the broadest national mandate.

※　　※　　※

The Commission's most difficult assignments have been **to uncover all the facts** concerning the assassination of President Kennedy and to **determine if it was in any way directed or encouraged by unknown persons at home or abroad.** . . . The task has demanded unceasing appraisal of the evidence by the individual members of the Commission in their effort to discover the whole truth.

The Warren Commission further stated:

No limitations have been placed on the Commission's inquiry; it has concluded its own investigation, and all Government agencies have fully discharged their responsibility to cooperate with the Commission in its investigation.

And,

> . . . if there is any . . . evidence [of conspiracy], it has been beyond the reach of all the investigative agencies and resources of the United States and has not come to the attention of this Commission.

In stark contrast, the most significant finding of the Select Committee was that:

> The Warren Commission failed to investigate adequately the possibility of a conspiracy to assassinate the President.

The Warren Commission was a "blue-ribbon" commission, designed to provide a convincing (believable) answer to the question of whether there was a conspiracy. It was headed by U.S. Supreme Court Chief Justice Earl Warren. Its members were U.S. Senator Richard B. Russell, U.S. Senator John Sherman Cooper, U.S. Congressional Representative Hale Boggs, Representative Gerald R. Ford (later to become President Gerald R. Ford), Mr. Allen W. Dulles (former Director of the CIA), and Mr. John J. McCloy (former president of the World Bank). J. Lee Rankin, former Solicitor General of the United States was appointed General Counsel, to head the staff of fourteen attorneys.

The purported mission of the Warren Commission was *not merely* to determine who may have pulled the trigger that unleashed the bullets that killed the president. Whether the bullets came from a Mannlicher-Carcano rifle that Lee Harvey Oswald had purchased, and whether he shot that rifle from the sixth floor of the Texas School Book Depository on November 22, 1963, were only the beginning issues. Our national security, our national well being, the confidence that the rest of the world would place in our government, and our own peace of mind as citizens, dictated that the more important issue was whether there was a conspiracy behind the assassination.

That the issue of conspiracy was not adequately investigated is even more troubling since the possibility of conspiracy so obviously could not have been rejected as being unworthy of serious consideration. The Russians, with whom Kennedy came to the brink of nuclear war; the Cubans, whose leader we attempted to assassinate; the displaced anti-Castro Cubans, who hated Kennedy for breaking his promise to help them reclaim their home land; the Mafia, who saw the Kennedy family as traitors whose organized crime program was destroying their existence; the right-wing extremists in the South, who hated Kennedy's liberal civil rights agenda; and, at least potentially, even elements of our own government, were all very real suspects, who undeniably considered Kennedy to be their enemy, hated him for what he had done, and feared him for what he proposed to do. And then there was Oswald, with his disturbing background and history of provocative associations; and Ruby—

Ruby, whose act in killing Oswald, alone, demanded that the possibility of conspiracy be thoroughly investigated.

So, was it a coverup?

There are various possible reasons why the Warren Commission failed to conduct an effective conspiracy investigation, including the one most often suspected, a criminal coverup of the government's own involvement. Most of such possible explanations, however, have never attained the status of real answers, since (at least to date) they have remained void of credible evidentiary support, and thus, are mere speculations.

The explanation that I believe is the real one, is that the Warren Commission had the *wrong attitude* about their responsibilities, and the objectives they should have been pursuing in their investigation. The fact that I say *attitude* was the main reason for the failure of the Warren Commission to conduct an effective conspiracy investigation may seem shocking, or perhaps even ridiculous. So let me explain.

Conspiracies, by their very nature, are secretive. In fact, they are commonly recognized as being a particularly dangerous kind of criminal activity in large part because their secretive nature makes them difficult to uncover. The Mafia is a classic example of conspiracy. The Mafia's long history of successful operation in various countries throughout the world (including the United States) illustrates the enormous dedication and perseverance that law enforcement has needed to penetrate its veil of secrecy.

Investigations of conspiracies rarely succeed when investigative bodies start with the preconceived attitude that the crime was probably committed solely by the perpetrator who is first apprehended—an attitude, for example, that the case should be closed upon the initial arrest of the truck driver who is apprehended transporting the contraband. Thus, just as it may be said that all of life is to some degree a self-fulfilling prophesy, it is particularly true in investigations that if you don't look for evidence of a conspiracy, if you don't really *want* to find it and look long and hard to find it, you are not going to find the evidence. (You may even disbelieve and reject it if it jumps out at you.)

But, you may say, shouldn't an investigative body keep an open mind, and impartially investigate the facts in order to be certain to fairly evaluate the evidence that is gathered? No, even though that sounds good, it simply doesn't work. Or, to state it differently, I don't believe that there is such a thing as a truly "open mind." Everyone starts out with some bias, some preconceived attitude about what is going to happen and what they will find, in life, and any undertaking in life. More often than not, they find exactly what they expect to find, exactly what they are looking for. Every juror in every trial has biases or preconceived attitudes. So does every parent, every investigator, and—yes—even every judge in our courts of law.

Further, contrary to common misconception, bias is

not limited to the slow witted or the uneducated, and it does not distort the thinking of only the slow witted or the less educated. Nor is bias limited to those who openly reveal their biases by their conduct. Racial prejudice, for example, is not limited to those who openly demonstrate their racial prejudices.

I am not suggesting that bias, in and of itself, is a bad thing. Everyone has biases which serve as the starting assumptions for approaching the everyday issues and tasks in our lives. Biases—at least in the sense that I am using the word—are as natural as the mental images you form of people who you have not yet seen. Such starting assumptions are typically generalizations, formed from your life experiences. They serve as a frame of reference, within which you take in new data and make decisions.

The problem seems to arise from the fact that biases are most often subconsciously formed, and they become imbedded in our minds without our making any deliberate choice or any conscious decision about their validity. They become particularly pernicious forces in our lives when we deny (or fail to recognize) their existence, and thus do not realize the subconscious effects they have upon our thinking. It is because of their typically *subconscious* role in our thinking that the word "bias" most often—and rightfully—has a negative connotation, denoting a preference or inclination that inhibits impartial judgment, or reflects unfairness or destructive prejudice. In a broader sense, however, a bias is not only a natural thing; it can be a very good thing, something that enhances our productivity and tends to lead to better outcomes in life. An example of such a good bias might be the starting assumption that "people of different skin color, nationalities, and religions are interesting, and my life is enhanced by meeting and becoming friends with people who do not look or dress or think exactly as I do." Such a good bias could be subconsciously formed from your experiences. Or, it could be consciously chosen—"adopted" by you. (There is nothing that necessarily prevents us from giving some thought to, or even consciously choosing our biases.)

Perhaps the greatest irony about biases is that they often seem to create the most havoc in highly educated and intelligent people. I do admit that I have had only limited experience with such people. Nevertheless, I have observed that it often seems easy for smart people to rationalize any position that they decide to take on an issue. I have also observed that smart people often start with the assumption that they are *above* having any significant biases, or at least, that they are above letting biases affect their thinking. Highly intelligent people tend to see themselves as being rational, and they know that any bias is at least partially irrational (since a bias is inherently a generalization). Their "bias" is that they are "above such irrationality."

Recognizing one's biases or preconceived attitudes usually tends to diminish the effect that the bias has upon rational analysis. For this reason, many trial lawyers in picking a jury do not assume that they can identify every potentially destructive bias of each juror, or that they have any chance of changing the juror's biases. Instead, they try to get the jurors to recognize their own biases so that in the serious performance of their responsibilities the jurors will consciously put their biases aside—at least to the extent of giving their client an even break by not rejecting all of the evidence in the case out of hand.

So, what does this long-winded dissertation have to do with the Warren Commission's investigation? As I stated above, the Warren Commission was a "blue-ribbon" commission whose members were selected for their reputations as intelligent, respected and honorable men. The obvious intention in forming a blue-ribbon commission was that its final report would be *believed,* and that the national concerns surrounding the assassination of President Kennedy could thereby be put to rest. The Warren Commission had the advantage of conducting its investigation close in time to the events being investigated. The Warren Commission spent four times as much money (in inflation-adjusted dollars) as the Select Committee spent.

Unfortunately, the record reflects that neither the intelligence, nor the stature, nor the prestige of the Commission's members, nor the timing, nor the amount of money spent, was sufficient to overcome the attitude with which the investigation was conducted. What was investigated, how it was investigated, what was "found" and what was "not found," I believe, were all the natural end result of what the Warren Commission wanted to find and did not want to find, almost as certainly as you can predict that if your gardener plants an acorn, what you will get is an oak tree, even though he promised you a rose garden.

The fact that preconceived attitudes can completely control one's evaluation of evidence relating to the Kennedy assassination was vividly illustrated in the Foreword to the reprint of the Select Committee's final report, which was published in paperback form by Bantam Books in July 1979. The Foreword was written by Tom Wicker, Associate Editor of THE NEW YORK TIMES. Mr. Wicker, obviously because he was a well-educated, respected, and intelligent man, was asked to review and comment on the Committee's Final Report. The Select Committee on Assassinations had just spent two and a half million dollars, and more than two years, gathering rooms full of testimony, documents, scientific tests and expert opinions. The issues were, Who killed the president, and was there a conspiracy? The evidence was laid out in the Committee's several hundred page main report, and twelve volumes of detailed supporting data. In the Report and supporting volumes, the Committee summarized and analyzed the evidence gathered in that investigation, and set forth the conclusions of the attorneys, researchers, investigators, and members of Congress who had reviewed that evidence. In the Foreword to that Report which Mr. Wicker was commissioned to write, he set forth his conclusion that there was no conspiracy, and that Lee Harvey Oswald acted alone. In other words, he reached the same conclusion as the Warren Commission, and rejected the conclusion of the Select Committee.

If I only described to you Mr. Wicker's *reason* for concluding that there was no conspiracy, you might not believe me. So here are his own words. After first admitting that he had studied the Committee's evidence and conclusions "only briefly," he stated the reason that he did not believe there was a conspiracy:

> *I do so not least because . . . I have always thought that Oswald acted alone when he killed Kennedy* (call it a stubborn refusal to face facts, if you insist); its obverse, I believe, is why so many Americans seem to want a conspiracy to have been responsible. A lonely, unstable young man, fiercely desiring recognition, bitterly angry at a world that denied it to him; a sudden opportunity to strike at that world by striking at another young man unfairly (as Oswald thought) granted immense recognition, immense power—*I believe that is the way things happen. Ours is a world not so much of plans and conspiracies but of chance, circumstance, and individuality, against which not even presidents can be always immune.*

Mr. Wicker's "evaluation" of all of the extensive work of the Select Committee was really not an evaluation at all. It was a rationalization: he reviewed the evidence—cursorily, as he admitted—in order to rationalize (i.e., to justify and not disturb) his preconceived attitudes about the way the world works. He believed that assassinations are carried out by lone nuts, and he found no difficulty in construing all the facts and evidence in accord with that preconception.

But the sad truth is that Mr. Wicker is not unusual. He is simply a convenient example of the control that our biases (our preconceived attitudes) have over our thought pro-

138

cesses. Tom Wicker only superficially reviewed the facts, the evidence, the testimony, the documents, and the analysis of those who had spent two years studying the issue. He really did not find the evidence to be of much interest at all. His ultimate "conclusion" or "finding" was nothing more or less than a self-fulfilling prophesy: what he found in the Select Committee's Report was what he started out looking to find.

Because of the almost inescapable influence of preconceived attitudes over what masquerades as impartial evaluation of the information that we all gather during our lives, I believe that the most critical, outcome-determinative factor in our endeavors is the attitude that we adopt in pursuing them. As a trial attorney, this is a particularly interesting phenomenon since it suggests that the single most important factor in trying a case is the selection of the jury—which unfortunately is also the most difficult thing to do.

But back to the point. Because attitude was the most important factor in determining the outcome of the Warren Commission's investigation, there was only one proper attitude for the Warren Commission to have had if the real object was to answer the question, Was President Kennedy killed as a result of a conspiracy? *Whether or not there was a conspiracy,* the only proper attitude, intention, and desire would have been to try to prove the existence of a conspiracy. *If* you proceed with that attitude, and if there was a conspiracy, and if you look in the right places, and if you are lucky and get the right breaks, you might then find (and actually *be able to see)* evidence of it. On the other hand, if the

Warren Commission started with the contrary attitude—the one that Mr. Wicker had—human nature and the difficulty of the job at hand predictably would have worked to assure that they did not find a conspiracy, even if one existed.

But *what evidence* is there that the Warren Commission did not want to find evidence of a conspiracy, if one existed? First, as we at the Select Committee proceeded through the first year of our investigation, our investigative efforts repeatedly revealed that the numerous conspiracy theories suggested over the years—theories such as those surrounding the "Umbrella Man," the "two-Oswald" theory, and the statistical basis for the "mysterious deaths" argument—were all factually flawed. Yet, even as we were systematically finding it necessary to reject those specific theories, it simultaneously became more and more obvious that there were great quantities of evidence suggesting real possibilities of conspiracy, evidence that either had not been investigated by the Warren Commission or had been rejected for insubstantial reasons by the Warren Commission.

The Warren Commission's repeated failure to pursue obvious avenues of investigation related to conspiracy issues and/or rejection of evidence that did come to their attention indicating possible conspiracy, was even more troubling in light of the fact that the Commission routinely pursued its investigation in a competent and aggressive manner whenever the question was whether Oswald fired upon the president from the School Book Depository. Oswald's conduct in purchasing the Mannlicher-Carcano rifle, and his activities im-

140

mediately before and after the assassination, seemed to have been of great interest to the Warren Commission; whether there was a conspiracy seemed to have been an annoyance.

The typical pattern of the conspiracy investigation both within the Commission itself, and within the FBI, who were the Warren Commission's investigators, was like this. Someone would come to the FBI and say that Mr. X was a close associate of Oswald. The FBI would pursue this lead until evidence discounting it was obtained. If Mr. X said he didn't know Oswald (which he was likely to do, whether or not he actually knew Oswald, since Oswald was believed to have shot the president, and no one really wanted to admit being associated with him), there was often nothing more done to pursue the issue. When more detailed witness interviews suggesting conspiracy did make it through the FBI filter, and were presented to the Warren Commission for evaluation, credibility issues were typically resolved in favor of the lone nut theory. A vivid example of such "evaluations" of witness credibility involved the Warren Commission's discounting of eyewitness reports from persons in Dealey Plaza. Appendix XII of the Warren Commission's Report, styled "Speculations and Rumors," contains a long list of what the Commission called "speculations" on the source of the shots, each of which is dismissed seriatim by cursory "Commission findings." The Select Committee reviewed much of the same evidence in its final Report. "The Committee noted that a significant number of witnesses reported that shots originated from the grassy knoll," and found that the testimony was not only consistent with the acoustics data that indicated a shot from the grassy knoll, but was also corroborated by photographic data and other evidence that was consistent with the witnesses' descriptions.

During our investigation, as I became more and more concerned with the Warren Commission's pattern of effectively investigating the question of whether Oswald was guilty, and the contrasting pattern of failing to pursue and/or discounting available evidence of conspiracy, I began questioning Warren Commission personnel, asking, Why did you conduct your investigation in this way? Why didn't you conduct an effective, aggressive conspiracy investigation? I questioned the former Solicitor General, J. Lee Rankin, who served as the Warren Commission's General Counsel. I also questioned Commission member Gerald Ford, and various attorneys that worked on the Commission's staff, among others. Perhaps not surprisingly, their typical response was somewhat defensive. Many of them flatly stated that they resented my accusations, and that the Warren Commission's work (i.e., *their* work) had been superb. Illustrative, was the testimony of former President Gerald Ford, who, in our public hearings, had this to say in response to my questions:

> Mr. Chairman and Mr. Cornwell, the committee did send to me this question, among others. . . . Because I want to be very accurate . . . I would like, if I might, Mr. Chairman, to read a response to the question that Mr. Cornwell has asked, and with your approval I will do so.
>
>   ❈   ❈   ❈

142

I categorically deny that the investigation of the assassination was deficient.

Then, one day I had the opportunity to question Nicholas deB. Katzenbach in a deposition in my office. Mr. Katzenbach, as you may recall, was the Deputy Attorney General under Robert Kennedy. After the assassination, Bobby Kennedy was devastated by his brother's death, and effectively ceased functioning as Attorney General. His Deputy, Katzenbach, took over the job of running the Justice Department. In addition, Katzenbach played a key role in the formation of the Warren Commission.

I first asked Mr. Katzenbach to describe the immediate problems that the government faced as a result of the assassination. He said:

> . . . there were questions of Oswald's visit to Russia, marriage to Marina and the visit to Mexico City, the question of whether there was any connection between Ruby and Oswald, how in hell the police could have allowed that to happen. . . . The question as it came along as the result of all those things was whether this was some kind of conspiracy, whether foreign powers could be involved, whether it was a right-wing conspiracy, whether it was a left-wing conspiracy, whether it was the right-wing trying to put the conspiracy on the left-wing or the left-wing trying to put the conspiracy on the right-wing . . . there were *many rumors* around. There were *many speculations* around, *all of which were problems.*

More specifically, though, *why* were such rumors and speculations a problem? Was it because it was difficult to decide how the conspiracy questions could be most effectively

143

investigated? Was it because he was concerned about the magnitude of the task of finding the evidence of conspiracy, if it existed? Katzenbach thought that the rumors and speculations were a problem for quite different reasons: the rumors and speculations were hampering their ability to get on with the job of running the government, and dealing with the world. Katzenbach wanted something he could give the State Department so they could convince foreign governments that Vice President Johnson had not gained the presidency through a coup, something to satisfy the American public, and something to prevent continual investigations and re-investigations. In short, as he saw it, the real problem was a public relations problem, both here, and abroad, and he wanted something everyone would believe:

> The thing that influenced me personally perhaps more than anything else was the Lincoln assassination and the fact that a century later people were still coming out with books about Lincoln, who was the real assassin, who conspired and so forth and so on. I thought it had foreign policy implications because of speculations about whether the Russians were behind this, could they have done this? Was it in retaliation for the Bay of Pigs? Finally, I think in terms of protecting President Johnson because people abroad in many countries, if they had a head of state assassinated, assumed that the person who succeeded him had something to do with it. . . . My hope, I guess naive in view of my testimony here today, was that . . . we would not be exposed to re-investigation as was the case with Lincoln, every five or ten or fifteen years whenever anybody was inspired to do it.

So, how did he believe the public relations problem could best be solved?

> I doubted that anyone in the government, Mr. Hoover, or the FBI, or myself or the President or anyone else, could satisfy a lot of foreign opinion that all facts were being revealed and that the investigation would be complete and conclusive and without any loose ends. So from the beginning, I felt that some kind of commission would be desirable for that purpose. . . . it would be desirable for the President to appoint some commission of people who had international and domestic public stature and reputation for integrity that would review all of the investigations and direct any further investigations. . . . As far as the particular people are concerned, I had not any great thoughts of particular people outside of the fact that if you do not want to have a separate House or Senate investigation, it would probably involve people of prestige from those two bodies and whatever other persons were acceptable and somebody of enormous prestige to head it. I thought that Chief Justice Warren probably had more credibility abroad than any other American at that particular time in history. . . . It was sort of hard to think of anybody who could serve that role better than he.

And what did Katzenbach believe the prestigious panel would tell the American public and the world? His thoughts on that subject were recorded in a memo he wrote to Bill Moyers, a special White House assistant to President Johnson, on Monday, November 25, 1963—just three days after the assassination. As Katzenbach saw it, the commission would *tell* the public—and use its prestige to *convince*

145

the public—that Oswald was the sole assassin. Here is the full memorandum:

November 25, 1963
MEMORANDUM FOR MR. MOYERS

It is important that all of the facts surrounding President Kennedy's Assassination be made public in a way which will satisfy people in the United States and abroad that all the facts have been told and that a statement to this effect be made now.

1. *The public must be satisfied that Oswald was the assassin; that he did not have confederates who are still at large; and that the evidence was such that he would have been convicted at trial.*

2. *Speculation about Oswald's motivation ought to be cut off, and we should have some basis for rebutting thought that this was a Communist conspiracy or (as the Iron Curtain press is saying) a right-wing conspiracy to blame it on the Communists.* Unfortunately the facts on Oswald seem about too pat—too obvious (Marxist, Cuba, Russian wife, etc.). The Dallas police have put out statements on the Communist conspiracy theory, and it was they who were in charge when he was shot and thus silenced.

3. The matter has been handled thus far with neither dignity nor conviction. Facts have been mixed with rumour and speculation. We can scarcely let the world see us totally in the image of the Dallas police when our President is murdered.

I think this objective may be satisfied by making public as soon as possible a complete and thorough FBI report on Oswald and the assassination. This may run into the difficulty of pointing to inconsistencies between this report and state-

146

ments by Dallas police officials. But the reputation of the Bureau is such that it may do the whole job.

The only other step would be the appointment of a Presidential Commission of unimpeachable personnel to review and examine the evidence and announce its conclusions. This has both advantages and disadvantages. I think it can await publication of the FBI report and public reaction to it here and abroad.

I think, however, that a statement that all the facts will be made public property in an orderly and responsible way should be made now. We need something to head off public speculation or Congressional hearings of the wrong sort.

Nicholas deB. Katzenbach
Deputy Attorney General

During Katzenbach's public testimony before the full Select Committee on Assassinations, Congressman Dodd stated, ". . . I am perplexed, absolutely perplexed, on why it was in the public interest to prove that Oswald was the one, and . . . did not have confederates who were still at large." Katzenbach responded in part by describing his memo to Moyers as not being "artistically phrased," and then added, "Perhaps you have never written anything that you would like to write better afterwards, Congressman, but I have."

Katzenbach also defended his memo by noting that it did contain language about making "all of the facts" public, and during his deposition in my office, he said several times that he wanted all of the facts to be ultimately made public.

147

But the memo contains no discussion about *uncovering* "all of the facts." Nor does it contain any suggestion as to whether the FBI, or the prestigious commission, or some other mechanism, would be best suited to uncover the facts. Instead, the memo merely sets forth the need to present the specified facts "*in a way which will satisfy people* in the United States and abroad."

The concluding (unnumbered) paragraphs of his memo are less blunt, but just as interesting. He suggests the possible formation of a "Presidential Commission of unimpeachable personnel," but notes that such a commission would have both "advantages and disadvantages," and that it might not even be needed. He never suggests that, even if created, it would *investigate,* but only that it would "review and examine the evidence and announce its conclusions." If it was not to investigate, but only to review, examine and announce, it seems, again, fairly obvious that its function would be solely to "convince" (presumably by the power of its prestige). And because the goal of "convincing" might be achieved simply by making an FBI report public as soon as possible—"the reputation of the Bureau is such that it may do the whole job"—the [Warren] commission alternative, in his view, might best "await publication of the FBI report." (If more were needed, the Commission could be formed to review and "bless" the FBI's conclusions.)

Katzenbach expressed his views not only to Bill Moyers, but also directly to President Johnson. He also talked to Dean Rusk and Alexis Johnson in the State Department, who were in agreement, although they were "very much interested in time. They wanted to get something out in a hurry. The State Department was constantly pressing because, I guess, of the rumors abroad or the accusations."

Within days, Johnson decided to form the Presidential Commission, and that Chief Justice Warren should head it. Katzenbach told me that when Johnson at first was not able to convince Chief Justice Warren to take the job, he asked Katzenbach to speak with the Chief Justice:

> Cornwell: What, if any, arguments did you use to try to persuade him?
> Katzenbach: Essentially the same ones I have given you now, that I thought that everything had to be done that would give public opinion all over the world confidence that the true facts had been revealed. . . . I thought it took a man of his prestige and experience to do it.

So, why was Katzenbach so ready and willing, only three days after the assassination, to conclude that Oswald was a lone assassin and that there was no conspiracy? Why was his focus upon getting the world to accept that conclusion, instead of the preliminary matter of determining if those really were the true facts? Why was speed so important? Katzenbach gave several explanations, the first being the pressures to provide an answer:

> I think my basic motivation was the amount of speculation both here and abroad as to what was going on, whether there was a conspiracy of the right or a conspiracy of the left or a

lone assassin or even in its wildest stages, a conspiracy by the then Vice President to achieve the Presidency, the sort of thing you have speculation about in some countries abroad where that kind of condition is normal. It seemed to me that the quicker some information could be made available that went beyond what the press was able to uncover and what the press was able to speculate about was desirable in that state of affairs.

⌗   ⌗   ⌗

I was certainly communicated with several times by the State Department and I suppose in a sense that is pressure, although I do not know that I really felt it as pressure. I felt they had their problems and they wanted some help in trying to resolve them. We have 120, or whatever it is, Embassies around the world and every Ambassador there was being asked about this, being asked by that government what was happening, what was the story on it, as well as what effect it would have on our foreign policy, and I think they were very—being no information really available to them, they were simply feeling the lack of it and feeling that affected their credibility in foreign governments.

⌗   ⌗   ⌗

I think I was pushing largely because the State Department was pushing me.

Katzenbach also suggested that the lone assassin explanation was not just expedient, it was *the FBI's* explanation:

> ... there is no investigative agency in the world that I believe compares with the Federal Bureau of Investigation then and I suppose it is probably true today.

⌗   ⌗   ⌗

> It was always my view, the whole time that I was in the Department of Justice, that the Bureau would do what you

150

asked the Bureau to do and that they would do it well and professionally.

⌗ ⌗ ⌗

It never would have occurred to me that the FBI would cover up anything.

Part of his explanation seemed to go beyond his trust of the FBI and his willingness to accept their conclusions. His testimony seems to indicate that he felt he had no other choice:

> You see, nobody really could do it [say what the investigation revealed] other than the Bureau, with the Bureau's acquiescence. Nobody else knew. I did not know what was going on. Nobody in the government knew what was going on other than very short conclusionary statements which you got from [FBI] liaison people, from the director himself. I did not know who they were interviewing or why they were interviewing, what they uncovered.
>
> ⌗ ⌗ ⌗
>
> . . . everybody [in the FBI] appeared to believe that Lee Harvey Oswald had acted alone fairly early.
>
> ⌗ ⌗ ⌗
>
> . . . very simply, if that was the conclusion that the FBI was going to come to, then the public had to be satisfied that was the correct conclusion.
>
> ⌗ ⌗ ⌗
>
> . . . you have got a lot of awkward facts that you are going to have to explain, and you had better explain them satisfactorily.

Several times in his testimony, Katzenbach said that he may have simply been naive in 1963. He said that he did not know of the CIA / Mafia plots to assassinate Castro; that those plots

151

had never been revealed to him or to the Warren Commission by either the CIA or the FBI; and that his recommendations would have been different if he had known then what he knows now:

> Katzenbach: It [the possibility that the CIA had been involved in plots to assassinate Castro] never occurred to me. Perhaps I was naive, but it never occurred to me. . . .
>
> ⚹ ⚹ ⚹
>
> Perhaps naively but I thought that the appointment of Allen Dulles to the Commission would ensure that the Commission had access to anything that the CIA had. I am astounded to this day that Mr. Dulles did not at least make that information available to the other commissioners.
>
> Apparently they [the FBI] were aware, if I read the report correctly, of some of the CIA activities, of at least the connection with the Mafia. That certainly should have been reported. I am very surprised that it was not. There was no love lost between the FBI and the CIA. I guess it must have been the FBI's view that they would have been as embarrassed as the CIA. . . .
>
> Cornwell: That brings me to the question, if you had known at that point in time what you now know or have reason to believe . . . that there were plots directed at Castro, that Hoover in fact was worried about internal repercussions . . . that the FBI at least in one small segment had destroyed a piece of evidence indicating on its face, maybe not in reality but at least on its face, the possibility of some association between the FBI and Oswald—there is, incidentally . . . a CIA memo which indicates that they had contemplated using Oswald as an agent—if you had known those types of things, been told them within a day or two of the assassination,

would you have opted for the early press release, early FBI report, that you had suggested?

Katzenbach: I do not think under those circumstances you could have. I think you would have had to say there is more here to sort out than we are now able to sort out. If I had known about those things, I would have said, "How are we going to cope with all this? We had better wait." I might add to that something I suppose is obvious, that those reasons were never given to me as reasons not to do this.

Whether Mr. Katzenbach gave us the *real* reasons for what he and our government did, or whether his reasons were actually only rationalizations for his adoption of the lone assassin theory, or whether he acted from other motives, I cannot say. It is always difficult to accurately assess what is in someone else's mind, even when you have the opportunity to ask them the question directly. In the end, we are often left to guess at intentions, *inferring* what we can from conduct.

I do believe that Nicholas Katzenbach accurately described what *happened* with the wheels of government in 1963 and 1964, even though why it happened may never be fully known. The evidence is quite clear that he and others put the machinery of government into gear to make the lone, deranged assassin story a convincing one. The Warren Commission's investigation, as well as its final Report, demonstrates clearly that it was, at best, an effort to accomplish precisely what Mr. Katzenbach said the government should do, convince the public that Oswald acted alone.

In its final Report, the Select Committee noted that:

- In the crucial areas of organized crime, Cuban exiles and other militant groups, and foreign complicity, the attorneys assigned were lacking in experience and knowledge. Moreover, there was little to indicate that outside experts in these areas were consulted.
- Neither the experience nor the approach of the Commission's staff was what should be expected in a criminal investigation.
- The Commission failed to use the legal tools available to it to pursue conspiracy issues, such as immunity from prosecution or prosecution for perjury with respect to witnesses whose veracity was questionable.
- The Commission chose not to hire its own investigators, but instead relied almost exclusively upon the investigation of the FBI, which was severely flawed for numerous reasons.
- The Commission merely "assumed" (erroneously) that the CIA would supply whatever information of relevance it had available. The CIA, in contrast, took the position that it should forward information only in response to specific requests, a position that resulted in significant quantities of information on numerous highly relevant subjects having never come to the Warren Commission's attention.
- The staff was initially hired on a short term, temporary basis, with the understanding that their work

would last for no more than 3 or 4 months, and that the investigation would be terminated by March, or April 1964, with a final report due by June 30. In fact, it was not until March that any real field work even commenced in Dallas, and mid-March before any investigation of Jack Ruby got underway. The result of pressures to complete the investigation eventually led to a number of senior staff counsel leaving their jobs with the Commission by the early summer of 1964, over 4 months before the investigation officially ended.

- In its final report, the Commission overstated the thoroughness of its investigation and the weight of its evidence, particularly in the area of conspiracy.

A detailed summary of the evidence that supports those conclusions is set forth in the 500 page staff report, published by the U.S. Government Printing Office as Volume XII of the Appendix to Hearings of the Select Committee on Assassination. That evidence, I believe, clearly proves that the Warren Commission was not sincerely interested in finding a conspiracy.

The kind of defects that pervaded its entire "search" for a conspiracy, are graphically revealed by even a cursory look at the Warren Commission's "organized crime investigation." Any true conspiracy investigation would have necessarily focused upon the Mafia as possible suspects. The Kennedy family had a long history of friendly and mutually beneficial business and political dealings with the Mafia, dating back to father Joseph Kennedy's business dealings and continuing through the machinations that got Jack Kennedy through tough elections in his rise to the presidency. Yet during the presidency of Jack Kennedy, his younger brother Bobby Kennedy had begun to run the Mafia out of business with the vigorous criminal prosecutions he headed as Attorney General of the Justice Department. From these known facts alone, one must suspect at least the possibility that the Mafia felt betrayed by the Kennedys, and sought some means of self preservation, if not revenge, in their traditional manner.

However, the Warren Commission conducted only a very limited investigation related to possible organized crime involvement. It focused its investigation exclusively on Jack Ruby. It did not investigate the possibility of involvement by the national crime syndicate in general, or individual leaders in particular. This was admitted by both J. Lee Rankin, the General Counsel to the Warren Commission, and Burt Griffin, the staff counsel who conducted the Ruby investigation. Griffin testified that ". . . the possibility that someone associated with the underworld would have wanted to assassinate the President . . . [was] not seriously explored" by the Commission. (Katzenbach said, "It would be wrong to act on the assumption that we thought organized crime had very much to do with the assassination.")

Among the available data ignored by the Warren Commission (and reviewed for the first time fifteen years later, by the Select Committee) were numerous tape recorded conversations by top level Mafia figures which the FBI had acquired through extensive illegal electronic surveillance of the Mafia in the years immediately preceding the assassination. In those conversations, top Mafia leaders repeatedly spoke of killing the president and/or his brother, the Attorney General.

The FBI was uniquely equipped to investigate the possibility of a Mafia conspiracy to kill the president, through its Special Investigative Division which had been formed two years earlier specifically to investigate organized crime. However, Former Assistant FBI Director Courtney Evans, who headed the Special Investigative Division, told us that the Warren Commission never consulted him or asked for any participation by his Division, stating "They sure didn't come to me. . . ." Nor did the Warren Commission employ the expertise of the Justice Department's organized crime section.

The FBI investigation was divided between two main divisions, the General Investigative Division and the Domestic Intelligence Division, and it was *the official in charge of the bank robbery desk* in the General Investigative Division who actually supervised the assassination investigation. The assistant FBI director in charge of the General Investigative Division testified that, while the Division was charged with investigating who specifically fired the shot or shots that killed President Kennedy, whether persons other than Oswald were involved was an "ancillary matter" that was not part of his division's responsibility. He characterized the investigation by saying, ". . . we were in the position of standing on the corner with our pocket open, waiting for someone to drop information into it...." And the former assistant director who coordinated the FBI's conspiracy investigation, in testimony before the Senate Select Committee to Study Governmental Operations with Respect to Intelligence Activities, characterized the Bureau's conspiracy investigation as rushed, chaotic, and shallow. In short, the possibility of Mafia involvement was never taken seriously. The Select Committee concluded that "conspiracy was a blind spot in the FBI's investigation," and the FBI was the Warren Commission's only investigative arm.

It is even more disturbing—just as with the Warren Commission itself—that the lack of effective conspiracy investigation by the FBI stood in stark contrast to their work which focused upon the guilt of Oswald. The Select Committee found that the overall investigation was "an effort of unparalleled magnitude:"

> In terms of hours worked, interviews conducted and tests performed, the FBI's response was in fact, unexcelled. . . . Over 80 Bureau personnel were sent to Dallas, over 25,000 interviews were conducted, and 2,300 reports, consisting of 25,400 pages were prepared.

Within this massive effort, it appeared to the Select Committee not only that "conspiracy was a blind spot in the FBI's investigation," but that "the FBI's investigation into a conspiracy was deficient in the areas that . . . were most worthy of suspicion, organized crime, pro- and anti-Castro Cubans, and the possible associations of individuals from these areas with Lee Harvey Oswald and Jack Ruby."

While we may never learn all of the underlying causes, the fact that this tragic investigation was the product of a wrong attitude is very clear. From the beginning there was pressure from FBI Director J. Edgar Hoover to complete the investigation in an unreasonably short period of time, and the overall investigation was obviously colored by Hoover's attitude that Oswald was a lone assassin. On November 24, 1963, the second day after the assassination, and just hours after Oswald had been shot and killed in the Dallas Police Department by Jack Ruby, Hoover had a telephone conversation with President Lyndon Johnson, in which Hoover said, "The thing that I am *most concerned about . . . is having something issued so we can convince the public that Oswald is the real assassin.*" Four days after the assassination, on November 26, 1963, Hoover received a memorandum from an assistant director stating that " . . . we must recognize that a matter of this magnitude cannot be fully investigated in a week's time." In a notation on the memo, Hoover responded, "Just how long do you estimate it will take. It seems to me we have the basic facts now."

Three days later, on November 29 — only one week after the assassination — Hoover recorded in a memorandum his conversation earlier that day with President Johnson:

I advised the President that we hope to have the investigation wrapped up today, but probably won't have it before the first of the week, due to an additional lead being pursued in Mexico.

Winding up the loose ends actually took another week. The FBI's report, setting forth its conclusions that Oswald, acting alone, had killed the President, was transmitted to President Johnson by Deputy Attorney General Katzenbach on December 9, 1963, just a little over one week after the Warren Commission was created.

It took the Warren Commission another nine months to "review and examine the evidence and announce its conclusions"—to use Katzenbach's words in his November 25 memo to Moyers. It is no surprise that during those months, Hoover and the Federal Bureau of Investigation, which he ran with an iron hand, never found any evidence that impeached their original conclusion that Oswald had acted alone.

As Katzenbach said, Hoover was "strongly opposed" to the creation of the Warren Commission, and considered the mere formation of the Commission to be a "slap at the Federal Bureau of Investigation"—"For Mr. Hoover, anything that was not lavish praise was terrible criticism, unjustified also." The FBI's response, according to Katzenbach, in large part was to stonewall the Commission, the Attorney General, and the Deputy Attorney General, and almost everyone else involved, adding that, "The Bureau during the time I was in the Department of Justice, had a very strong view that *they* were to do investigations."

The Bureau was also notorious for justifying their own acts and never admitting their shortcomings. In his deposition, Katzenbach illustrated the point by recounting a story. "We used to joke about it. I tell you once an agent was driving me out to the airport at LaGuardia and he missed a turn. I said to him, 'Have you missed a turn?' He looked at me. He said, 'No.' I said, 'You have.' He said, 'Do you not know that the Bureau can make no mistake.' Whereupon he did a 'U' turn and went back."

Would the FBI have even given the Warren Commission any conspiracy information, impeaching their preliminary conclusion that Oswald acted alone, had such information jumped into their laps? According to Katzenbach, only God may know:

What would have happened if they came across that kind of information, God only knows. What the reverberations of that in the FBI would have been, again, speaking of the FBI talking about minor embarrassment—in really uncovering something that would have changed some result they had reported, God only knows.

I think people's heads would have rolled and they would have swallowed hard and done it. I think my view at the time would have been that in a matter as important as the assassination of a president, I think the Bureau would have swallowed and taken it and found some graceful way out. Explaining why they had come to the wrong conclusion would have been a fairly high-powered neutron bomb in the Bureau, questioning any basic conclusion that they had come to.

Of course, the reason only God knows what they would have done with such evidence is that the question is largely hypothetical. They never looked for such evidence, and thus (apparently) never found it, so they never had to face the difficult decision of whether to disclose it. In the end, what the FBI provided to the Warren Commission was what the FBI looked to find; and the Commission, in turn, did its part to address what Hoover said he was "most concerned about," they issued a Report to "convince the public that Oswald is the real assassin."

The Warren Commission's final report proclaims that:

> No limitations have been placed on the Commission's inquiry; it has concluded its own investigation, and all Government agencies have fully discharged their responsibility to cooperate with the Commission in its investigation.

The Select Committee described that assertion as "an inaccurate portrayal of the [Warren Commission's] investigation."

On the issue of conspiracy, the Warren Commission stated:

> . . . if there is any . . . evidence [of conspiracy], it has been beyond the reach of all the investigative agencies and resources of the United States and has not come to the attention of this Commission.

The record of the Warren Commission's performance belies that representation.

There are many things that will never be known with certainty about the Kennedy investigation, but one thing that can be stated with utmost confidence is that it is impossible to rely upon the Warren Commission's conclusion that there was no conspiracy. Congressman McKinney asked Katzenbach during our public hearings whether, if the FBI and CIA had been cooperative and open to the Warren Commission, the Commission would have reached a different conclusion. In response, Katzenbach said, "I suppose one has to say, an investigation that did not take place, it is impossible to know what would have come out of it."

The Select Committee concluded its analysis of the Warren Commission's performance with these words:

> In conclusion, the committee found that the Warren Commission's investigation was conducted in good faith, competently, and with high integrity, but that the Warren Report was not, in some respects, an accurate presentation of all the evidence available to the Commission or a true reflection of the scope of the Commission's work, particularly on the issue of possible conspiracy in the assassination. *It is a reality to be regretted that the Commission failed to live up to its promise.*

I cannot dispute the Committee's conclusion about the Warren Commission's "good faith." We found no evidence of any deliberate wrongdoing, or intentional coverup. But the tragedy is no less a tragedy because it resulted from a wrong (good faith) attitude, than it would be if it had been the deliberate product of intentional bad faith. The result is identical.

*Weren't there political pressures
on the Select Committee?
After all, wasn't it a
Committee of Congress!*

Yes, some of the Committee members felt political pressure. In fact, one comical reflection of the obvious political realities occurred in the executive committee session at which the acoustics evidence was first presented to the Committee. Immediately upon hearing that the tests indicated that two gunmen had fired upon the president (and thus, that there was a conspiracy), one of the committee members jokingly got up from the table, put his briefcase under his arm, and said to the Chairman, "It's been good working with you, Lou, but I am going to have to go on to other affairs of Congress now!" Shortly afterward, this event was made the subject of a nationally published cartoon by the famous cartoonist, Pat Oliphant. The cartoon—a copy of which still hangs on my wall—portrays exactly what really happened. It shows the Select Committee, in the closed committee room, being presented with a paper captioned "Conspiracy Evidence" The title under the cartoon reads, "We have some Highly Inconvenient News." (I never knew who may have told Oliphant about the event.)

But I never saw or heard of any member of the Select Committee taking any action to guide or sway the investigative efforts of the staff. I believe that this was an unusual committee in many ways, but one fortunate bit of its uniqueness was that the staff was given the freedom to conduct the investigation, and to publish the evidence we gathered. The only time that I saw the effects of what might be described as "political thinking" was in the choice of words that were used in describing the degree of strength or certainty of the findings in the final Report, although I personally believe the choice of those words is probably better described as candor, than politics. Whereas the Warren Commission erred in overstating the certainty of its conclusions, the Select Committee consciously tried to err on the side of understating the strength of its conclusions. Although that "toned down" wording could be described as the "politically correct" thing to do, it seems to me to have been more the recognition of the inherent limitations under which we operated. We were, after all, a congressional investigation, whose processes are not intended to reach definitive conclusions about criminal activity, but rather to investigate in order to formulate recommendations for legislative changes. It would have been dishonest to characterize the "findings" from the investigation as being definitive, or beyond question.

Within those parameters, the final Report of the Select Committee fairly describes the evidence and what appeared to the Committee to be reasonable conclusions or findings based upon that evidence. Given the disclosure of the underlying evidence, the Committee's conclusions actually become even less important—for everyone is free and welcome to draw their own conclusions from the evidence.

What was the Select Committee's Focus?

One significant aspect of the answer to that question, obviously, is that in contrast to my need to infer the attitude of the Warren Commission from its actions, I don't need to look at circumstantial evidence to determine *my* attitude, or focus, or "bias" in supervising the Select Committee's investigation. Before joining the Select Committee, I had been a federal prosecutor with the Organized Crime and Racketeering Section of the Justice Department, and Chief of the Organized Crime Strike Force in Kansas City. I had investigated numerous conspiracies, and indicted and tried the organized crime members who participated in those conspiracies, including the head of the Mafia in Kansas City, and the head of the Mafia in Denver. I believe that criminal conspiracies do exist. Unlike Tom Wicker, my bias ran toward a belief that conspiracies are a very integral part of "how the world works." When I took the job with the Select Committee, I very much wanted to find a conspiracy in the Kennedy case if one existed.

And though perhaps no group of workers ever proceeds with identical attitudes about a job, even when they work together to achieve a common goal, I believe that the staff of the Select Committee wanted to find evidence of a conspiracy, if it existed. I cannot speak with as much knowledge about the attitudes of the congressmen who sat on the Committee, but perhaps my lack of knowledge about their attitudes is a revealing fact in and of itself. Whatever their preconceived attitudes may have been about what they hoped the Committee would uncover or not uncover, they showed the professionalism and good judgment not to attempt to impose those thoughts on the investigative staff. The staff was allowed to conduct the investigation, and to present whatever came of that investigation to the Committee, and through the Report and supporting volumes, to the public for their final evaluation. In the end, the Committee reviewed the evidence that we were able to gather, and announced the findings that they believed were justified by that evidence. I personally believe that those findings were honestly reached, and consistent with the evidence.

I also believe that it is significant that the members of the Select Committee who disagreed with the Committee's findings as set forth in the principal Report, published their disagreements in separate remarks, views and dissents. Every member of the Warren Commission indicated complete agreement with the entire Warren Report. In a case as complex as the Kennedy investigation, does it trouble you that no one on the Warren Commission disagreed with anything in the final Report? It certainly seems suspicious to me.

What did you think about the film JFK,
by Oliver Stone?

First, I loved watching the movie, and Kevin Costner,
Tommy Lee Jones, Donald Sutherland, Joe Pesci and Sissy
Spacek are among my favorite actors. (On the other hand,
my wife, Lynne, says that I have never seen a movie that I
didn't love—an assertion which is clearly an exaggeration,
but which I must admit does have a kernel of truth in it, and
in response to which I have often offered in my own defense
the theory that I am a trial lawyer and that "all great trial
lawyers love movies," as they must, for they are basically actors themselves.)

The movie is based upon the story of New Orleans
District Attorney Jim Garrison, who investigated the Kennedy case between 1967 and 1969, and ultimately charged
and tried a New Orleans businessman named Clay Shaw

with complicity in the assassination. The case against Shaw was at best circumstantial, and consisted mainly of his alleged association with Lee Harvey Oswald, anti-Castro militant and underworld associate, David Ferrie, and other right-wing extremists who worked in and around New Orleans in the summer of 1963. Shaw was acquitted.

The movie's basic premise was that Kennedy was killed as the result of a conspiracy involving the federal government. The movie was great entertainment, and thought-provoking if not profoundly disturbing to most people who saw it; but was the movie accurate? Its extensive use of real names, real places, and real events certainly convinced a lot of people that it was a portrayal of the truth.

Much of the movie actually did portray historical facts—or more precisely, evidence—accurately. And the movie to a great extent captured the "essence" of the Kennedy case by vividly displaying the huge array of conspiracy theories that have surrounded the case, and portraying the great breadth and complexity of the case. But the movie did not simply display the available evidence. It systematically interlaced dissected pieces of evidence with imaginings in order to create the appearance of "facts" which in truth rested upon nothing but unsupportable innuendo. Similarly, the movie did not simply display, but actually relied upon and promoted many of the historical conspiracy theories that investigation has shown to be without evidentiary support. The movie is probably worth discussing in some detail simply because, in these respects, it provides the most recent and widely consumed example of the promotion and perpetuation of the misunderstandings and misinformation that have so long surrounded the case. If we take the time to analyze it, and do not merely uncritically accept the conclusions it proffers for our consumption, the movie can actually teach us a lot about the Kennedy case.

Let's begin by stepping back, and looking at the overall structure of the movie. The central thesis of the movie—that the federal government, or at least a large number of the leaders in our federal government, killed our president—rested upon essentially three premises. The first premise or body of "proof" was that the federal government's original 1963–64 investigation of the question of conspiracy was a demonstrable farce. In support, the movie offers examples of events (many of which as portrayed are actually consistent with the evidence) reflecting suspicious events that were never pursued or were investigated poorly by the government in 1963–64. With the basic factual premise, there is (quite unfortunately) little room for disagreement. But isn't there, honestly, more than one possible conclusion that rationally can be drawn from that fact besides the one the movie would have us accept? Is the only logical conclusion that a failure to adequately investigate proves complicity, or a coverup? Among various other possibilities, the original investigation could have been mishandled due to bureaucratic bungling, incompetence, inexperience and/or naivete of those who conducted the investigation, or benign (as opposed to sinister) biases and preconceived notions about the world (e.g., the belief that coup d'etat's don't happen in the United States, and thus, such a possibility simply did not merit investigation). The failure to adequately investigate may support a suspicion of government coverup, but more is certainly needed to reach such a conclusion.

Second, the movie asks us to conclude that the federal government must have killed our president because there is no proof that the federal government killed our president. Once again, the factual premise is correct, but the logic is faulty, since it assumes that there is no proof that the federal government killed the president because the federal government conducted the investigation and destroyed the proof. Suffice it to say that this reasoning is circular at best, and fairly constitutes no proof at all. Such thinking, in fact, was the approach taken in the Salem witch trials in 1692, where the absence of any evidence that the accused was a witch was sufficient for conviction. (Even for purposes of movies, we perhaps should have moved beyond such "logic" over the course of the past three hundred years.)

Third, as its last prong of "proof" the movie offers "confidential information" provided by the "former head of Black Ops" (a purported intelligence agency officer played by Donald Sutherland), who is shown meeting in Washington, D.C. with New Orleans District Attorney Jim Garrison (played by Kevin Costner). The Sutherland character tells Garrison on a "confidential basis" that he (Garrison) "is close, closer than you know" to unraveling the massive federal government conspiracy that was behind the death of the president. The Donald Sutherland character refuses to give Garrison his name and refuses to testify. And even though Garrison indicates that he really has no evidence, he tells Garrison to go forward with his criminal prosecution—"to keep stirring the pot" with the hope that the government will ultimately crack!

Is it just because I am a trial lawyer, or do you also think it is a little offensive to ask us to believe that our government is run not merely by criminals, but in fact by murderers, whose power over us was gained by a massive conspiracy to commit treason by killing the president, all upon the sole basis of a witness who never appeared at Garrison's trial and was not subject to cross-examination? But even that is not all. Garrison never actually went to Washington, and never spoke to the Donald Sutherland character, in person or over the telephone, during his actual investigation. From all accounts, the meeting and the conversation were simply figments of Oliver Stone's imagination.

One irony of all of this lies in the parallels between the movie and real life. The Warren Commission told the American public that the federal government had done everything in its power to find a conspiracy, and tried to convince us that because they found no conspiracy, it was clear that Lee Harvey Oswald acted alone. What the Warren Commission told us was quite simply not the truth, in that they simply did not have any real evidence to support their conclusion. Oliver Stone—just like his protagonist Garrison had done before him—then told us that there was a conspiracy, and that the federal government was behind it, and used all of his considerable powers to convince us of that fact. But that assertion was just as devoid of supporting evidence as the assertion of the Warren Commission.

But, you may say, what does a movie really have to do with the Kennedy case anyway? Aren't the standards different, and doesn't everyone recognize the difference between the government and a movie? The Warren Commission, after all, was part of our government, and thus *supposed* to tell us the truth. Movies are just movies. But do we tend to trust one more than the other, and if so, is it the government or the movies? Upon which do we more often rely in forming our views of the world? Does our government, or the media have a greater effect on us in shaping our thoughts and our decisions? True, we know that some movies are pure fiction, but did Oliver Stone present the movie *JFK* as pure fiction? Weren't you led to believe that the portrayal of events in *JFK* was based on fact? In the interviews that Stone gave about the movie, he clearly indicated that he personally believed the federal government killed Kennedy, and that he wanted to convince the public of that fact. But the average moviegoer does not have the power, the money, and the resources that were available to Oliver Stone to investigate the facts. And doesn't *the power to convince* have some measure of responsibility associated with it, even when the power to influence does not derive from our *tax* dollars?

But maybe the federal government *was* involved! What about every citizen's right—including Oliver Stone's right—in a free society to suggest that possibility? Just because no solid evidentiary support has ever been developed to support the theory that the federal government killed President Kennedy, obviously does not mean that the federal government was not involved. It is certainly true that no one has ever proven that the federal government, or even some rogue members of it, were not involved. The Warren Commission said they proved that fact, but that was not the truth: they didn't even look very hard for such proof. And the Select Committee looked and found nothing, but we were fifteen years late, and proving a negative (that there was no involvement) is difficult even under the best of circumstances. Finally, we would indeed be foolish to reject such a possibility out of hand, or to assume that our country is immune to coup d'etats.

To this limited extent, the movie's thesis was correct. We not only must remain vigilant to such a possibility, if we are to protect our freedoms, but in addition, there were many concrete reasons to ask the question in the Kennedy case. Oswald's long history of contradictory political activities, his military background coupled with his defection to Russia and his travel to Mexico just before the assassination, his known associations with people who had intelligence community ties, and the farcical investigation of conspiracy issues in 1963–64, all cry out for explanations. Notwithstanding his other shortcomings, even Jim Garrison (during the early stages of his investigation) uncovered evidence suggesting why the issue of possible government involvement

175

merited investigation. For these and the other reasons indicated in the movie, the possibility of government involvement not only merited, but required investigation in 1963– 64, and again in 1977–78 by the Select Committee on Assassination—arguably, perhaps, even by the District Attorney in New Orleans in 1967– 69. But having reasons to investigate is not the same thing as having evidence upon which to draw ultimate conclusions.

If it can be said that the Warren Commission acted irresponsibly in telling us that there was no conspiracy without having any real factual basis for that assertion, wasn't it just as irresponsible for the New Orleans District Attorney to prosecute charges of conspiracy without any substantial evidence of criminal culpability? And wasn't it irresponsible for Oliver Stone to try to convince us that our governmental leaders engaged in treason and murder by fabricating events and presenting them in a way to give them false credibility?

My point, however, is not simply to criticize. Since this is, hopefully, a book about history, the real question is, Can we learn something from the movie about what causes such irresponsibility—maybe, even something about what has generally caused such irresponsibility to plague the search for real answers in the Kennedy case for the past 35 years? Actually, one of the best reasons to watch the movie is for the great insight it provides into this issue.

What the movie reveals is the corrupting influence of the loss of objectivity. As portrayed in the movie, District

Attorney Jim Garrison vividly illustrates the intensity of feeling that so often consumes people who become involved in studying the Kennedy case, and the distortions in perception and aberrant behavior that such intensity seems to produce. In the movie, Garrison quite simply became obsessed with the case. His wife told him that he loved the case more than his family, but it went far beyond the case merely taking Garrison away from his family. His obsession caused him to lose sight of his responsibilities as a lawyer, and in his quest for real answers he lost sight of the value of truth. His obsession started, as is often the case, from realizing the undeniable fact that our government clearly botched the original investigation in 1963–64. From that realization, grew a mind-boggling array of questions, issues, doubts and, eventually, paranoia and loss of perspective—all of which was (perhaps) predictable, if not inevitable, and (unfortunately) not unique, for what happened to Garrison is only distinguishable in degree of magnitude from what has so frequently happened to those who study the case.

How could our government do such a bad job, and what in the world could have prompted them? In the end, Garrison went off the deep end. Garrison became obsessed with the issues, and after his principal suspect, David Ferrie, mysteriously died in the middle of the investigation, the lack of evidence was an insufficient deterrent to keep Garrison from proceeding to trial. As so often has happened to others, Garrison succumbed to the temptation to fill the void in real answers with his own pet theory. (He lost sight of the need for evidence to play the central role when he wrote the script for his play.)

In the end, at a meeting in his home attended by Garrison's wife and staff members, Garrison tacitly admits that he has insufficient evidence to convict Clay Shaw of any wrongdoing, but rationalizes his conduct in prosecuting Shaw as the "first step" to bring *the truth* to the attention of the American public "even if it takes another twenty-five or thirty years." Then, in an eloquent closing argument to the jury, Garrison espouses grand notions of justice, artfully uses unanswered issues to paint the specter of conspiracy, and decries the public's inability to learn the full truth. But the closing argument reveals as much by what it did not include—any description of evidence showing that Shaw was involved in the assassination—as by what it did include. In his plea for the jury to focus on higher ideals of truth and justice, Garrison simply lost site of the fact that his own prosecution lacked any justice, for it was devoid of any real evidence that the defendant Shaw was involved in the assassination of the president.

The movie excuses the fact that Shaw was prosecuted without evidence, by portraying Garrison as a brave crusader who fought against insurmountable obstacles created by the federal government, and who is worthy of our esteem as "the only man who ever brought to trial any charges in the Kennedy case." In the United States, because of our faith in the jury system as a means of "resolving" issues, we are often not satisfied until we receive a "concrete" or "definitive" answer in the form of a jury verdict. We also tend to admire those who provide us with that satisfaction—the lawyers, the judges, and the juries who render those answers—whether they are truly worthy of our admiration, or not. But Garrison proved nothing by bringing to trial a case that lacked substantial proof of actual complicity on the part of the charged defendant, and there is a difference between fighting to expose wrongdoing and bringing unfounded criminal charges.

In a tag line at the end of the movie, Stone reports that "In 1979, Richard Helms, Director of Covert Operations in 1963, admitted under oath that Clay Shaw had worked for the CIA." The obvious suggestion was that this admission proved that Garrison was on the right track, if not totally justified in charging Clay Shaw with killing the president, but in reality it was simply more innuendo, completely devoid of the kind of substance that would justify *any* conclusion about guilt or innocence. It was simply more of what both Garrison's closing argument, as well as the movie itself, consisted of.

Just like Garrison's argument to the jury, what this tag line tells us about the movie comes more from what it did not say, than what it did. If Stone knew what Helms testified to, why didn't he tell us? Why didn't he tell us what Helms said about *when* Shaw worked for the CIA? Did Helms testify that it was during the summer of 1963 when Oswald was in New Orleans, or years earlier? Did Shaw work as a CIA employee, or was he only an outside contact, someone whom the CIA periodically contacted and secured information from? For what division of the CIA did he work, and on what projects? Did Stone omit the details of Helms' testimony because those details did not support his premise (or Garrison's prosecution theory) that Clay Shaw was working for the CIA *in the summer of 1963,* and that whatever he did for the CIA had something to do with his contacts with Oswald, and that the "something" in turn was connected to the assassination that occurred a few months later?

Maybe Stone decided that these details are not important. But if those details are not important, then he is obviously asking us to believe that the mere fact that Shaw worked for the CIA—at any point in his life—makes him presumptively guilty in the assassination of President Kennedy (and if that is his logic, then perhaps he also believes that everyone who has ever worked for the CIA is presumptively guilty of killing the president). Or maybe Stone decided that even though the details of Helms' testimony were not helpful to his theory about CIA involvement in the assassination, Helms was lying about the details—you know, that Helms had given a "sanitized, half-truth" in his sworn testimony—so it was O.K. for Stone to just give us the "good" parts of Helms' testimony![1]

---

[1] I was intrigued by Stone's tag line, and made some inquiries which revealed that Stone's apparent source of information was a deposition given by Helms in a private civil lawsuit in Florida. I have not been able to review a copy of the actual testimony given by Helms in that deposition. However, the historical govern-

Again, what does this teach us about the Kennedy case? It historically has been such innuendo, calling for unjustified inferences and assumptions about the missing evidentiary detail, upon which the popular theories surrounding the case have historically been constructed. Such use of innuendo was not invented by Oliver Stone, nor is his movie necessarily even one of the worst examples. The movie does indicate that, sadly, some things never seem to change. The Warren Commission seemed to feel that "the national interests" provided sufficient justification to ignore the possibility of conspiracy, to try to convince the public that Oswald was a lone nut without regard to the facts or the evidence, and to withhold from the public those messy details that we could not be trusted to understand. Garrison seemed to feel that the long-term national interests "in getting at the truth" were sufficient justification for him to ignore his lack of real evidence and prosecute essentially unfounded criminal charges even without the evidence. And Oliver Stone seemed to feel that his personal agenda was sufficiently important to sell the story he wanted to sell without regard to the facts or the evidence, that he could fabricate whatever events were necessary to rewrite history and fill in the gaps in proof, and that whenever the available evidence didn't fit his precon-

ment memoranda that have been made public reflect that Shaw provided information to the CIA's Domestic Contact Service's New Orleans Office between 1948 and 1956, but that the CIA probably had no contact with him after 1956 with the exception of the occasion of a speech in 1961, when General Cabell, the Deputy Director of CIA, spoke before the Foreign Policy Association in New Orleans, and Shaw, who was the program director, introduced Cabell.

ceived scenario he was justified in withholding it from us—since we could not be trusted to evaluate it ourselves.

The final irony is that lack of honesty and candor about the basic issue of conspiracy has caused such grave doubts about the Warren Commission Report, the Garrison investigation, and the movie, that they have often been rejected wholesale—even the parts of each that were well founded. For us, perhaps the best that can be learned from the film is not to uncritically accept the conclusions and theories about the Kennedy case that have been and probably always will be offered in news articles, television documentaries, movies, and government investigations, for if we choose to swallow such conclusions whole, we will have mainly ourselves to blame for the resulting indigestion.

What is A Real Answer?

In contrast to the Warren Commission's, Jim Garrison's, and Oliver Stone's willingness to abandon the evidence in order to convince us of "their truth," there is a passage in the middle of the Report by the Select Committee on Assassinations that I believe captures the restraint that is necessarily an integral part of any true search for real answers. This particular passage was written to sum up the disturbing new evidence that the Committee had developed on the sinister appearing associations of Jack Ruby and Lee Harvey Oswald:

> The significance of the organized crime associations developed by the committee's investigation speaks for itself, but there are limitations that must be noted.
>
> ▷   ▷   ▷
>
> The evidence that has been presented by the committee demonstrates that Oswald did, in fact, have organized crime

associations. Who he was and where he lived could have come to the attention of those in organized crime who had the motive and means to kill the President. Similarly, there is abundant evidence that Ruby was knowledgeable about and known to organized crime elements. Nevertheless, the committee felt compelled to stress that knowledge or availability through association falls considerably short of the sort of evidence that would be necessary to establish criminal responsibility for a conspiracy in the assassination.

⌘　⌘　⌘

While the search for additional information in order to reach an understanding of Oswald's actions has continued for 15 years, and while the committee developed significant new details about his possible organized crime associations, particularly in New Orleans, the President's assassin himself remains not fully understood. The committee developed new information about Oswald and Ruby, thus altering previous perceptions, but the assassin and the man who murdered him still appear against a backdrop of unexplained or at least not fully explained, occurrences, associations and motivations.

The scientific evidence available to the committee indicated that it is probable that more than one person was involved in the President's murder. That fact compels acceptance. And it demands a reexamination of all that was thought to be true in the past. Further, the committee's investigation of Oswald and Ruby showed a variety of relationships that may have matured into an assassination conspiracy. Neither Oswald nor Ruby turned out to be "loners" as they had been painted in the 1964 investigation. Nevertheless, the committee frankly acknowledged that it was unable firmly to identify the other gunman or the nature and extent of the conspiracy.

Real answers inherently are honest answers, and honesty requires the restraint not to assert as "facts" that which is only suspicion—that which is not reasonably supported by available credible evidence.

In the beginning, it is necessary to start with the right attitude. I am critical of the Warren Commission for not wanting to find a conspiracy. Jim Garrison clearly wanted to find a conspiracy, yet I am also critical of his investigation, not for where or how it started, but for where it ended. In the end, real answers require more than a desire to look, they also require candor and objectivity. Sometimes the real answer is simply that we don't know for sure what the answer is.

A "real answer" also recognizes and acknowledges the limitations of our ability to know the ultimate truth. As the Select Committee gathered more and more data, I gradually came to realize that every presumed "fact" can be, and perhaps in some sense should always be, questioned. From the investigation, I came to recognize that, often, the more you study an issue and the more evidence you gather, the more clearly you are able to see how much you do not know.

Isn't it often those who know little who presume they know it all? Even the most basic "facts" that govern our lives—the "truths" upon which we were raised—concerning health and illness, mind and body, and even life and death, are still in the process of being reshaped by the latest scientific and medical discoveries, and the religious and philosophical thinkers of our day. If it were not for our belief

185

that we already have the answers, real "knowledge" would clearly progress even more rapidly. But somehow, we seem to overlook this lesson in studying history. We tend to hold fast to what we think we know, and resist admitting that we may have long been wrong, and need to think again.

During the course of the investigation, I acquired a small plaque on which is engraved the inscription, "A fact merely marks the point at which we have agreed to let investigation cease." That is the ultimate truth that studying the Kennedy case can teach you. Did Oswald fire the shots that killed the president? I believe that the real answer is yes, at least if you define "real answers" to mean those that are indicated by the evidence we have available to us at the point where we agreed to allow investigation to cease. Within that definition, I believe that the real answer is that there was a conspiracy, and that there were two shooters who fired at the presidential limousine. Those, of course, may or may not be the points at which you decide to let investigation cease.

Why are so many people
fascinated with the Kennedy case?

I think there are numerous reasons for the continued fascination. I am asked questions about the Kennedy case by almost everyone that I meet, and as soon as I start to answer the first question, more questions pop out. People seem to be thrilled with the possibility of hearing "the real answers" (although they often start with a different concept than I, about what "a real answer" is, wanting—as we all would like—to hear the "ultimate truths"). There have been over a thousand books written, mostly with theories about who did it, and new ones appear every year. Every year there is a continual stream of newspaper and magazine articles, and new web sites on the Internet, displaying and discussing the testimony of witnesses and other evidence, and the oldest and newest theories. The intensity of interest varies from that of people who have devoted *years* of their adult lives cataloging, studying and disseminating evidence and theories on the case—sometimes for profit, but even more often, just as a life-long hobby—to those who were not born until after the assassination, and are just becoming interested as they come to understand something about the case. (When I told my ten-year-old daughter, Josie, that I was thinking about writing this book, she was immediately interested. As she put it, "Oh, that sounds great! One of my friends in school knows all about the case, and told me about it!")

My own interest has never been at or near the obsessive level (except, of course, during the time that I ran the investigation for the Select Committee, when it was a fifteen-hours-a-day, six-days-a-week undertaking). I don't recall reading much about the subject, and certainly had not studied the evidence or theories, before I joined the Committee in 1977. I have spoken publicly about the case a few times over the years since 1979, generally at Chamber of Commerce meetings or other local gatherings in response to requests from friends. I wrote one article which was printed in the Congressional Record, appeared once on the Today show when Bryant Gumble did a fifteen minute spot on the case, provided some material for one chapter in someone else's book, gave my friend and former law partner, Bob Blakey, some minor assistance in proofing his book (*The Plot to Kill The President*) which was published in 1981, and appeared on two or three brief television and radio shows. But I admit that I have not closely followed, much less been actively involved in all of the continuing research and evaluation of "newly discovered" evidence and new conspiracy theories.

I suppose that my interest in the case has continued in part simply because it is fun to tell people about the case whenever they ask. My interest has also been professional, as a lawyer. The case is perhaps the most fascinating case that a lawyer could ever hope to work on, I am proud to have been given the opportunity to supervise the investigation for the Select Committee, and I am proud of the work that the Select Committee did. The investigation had its limitations, including time and monetary budgets within which the work had to be completed, and the extraordinary challenge of having to conduct a murder investigation fifteen years after the crime was committed, but I believe that the investigation was competently conducted, and that it provided a great service to the American people. At least in my "unbiased" opinion, it stands as the most thorough and honest overall investigation of the subject that has ever been done, and—simply because of the practical constraints imposed by the passage of years—that probably ever will be done.

The reasons for continued public interest are perhaps as varied as the personalities of people—the case seems to have something for everyone. Continued interest is certainly explained in part by feelings of personal loss. Kennedy's energy, good looks and charisma, coupled with his young age and the violence of his death, produced an outpouring of feelings that, if not unique, have perhaps only been equaled in modern history by the feelings associated with the death of Princess Diana. In all of the hundreds of conversations I have had with people over the years, the most common refrain has been, "I can still remember where I was when I heard the news." It is undoubtedly the associated emotions that cause memories to stick in our minds—they are really saying, "I can still remember *how I felt* when I heard the news."

Continued interest probably comes in part from new books on the subject. I personally believe that is good; it is an event worth being reminded of. It is a shame that the final Report of the Select Committee on Assassinations, which still contains the best overall description of the principal evidence and theories, is not generally available in libraries and book stores. More people should also read the Warren Commission Report, which is generally available in libraries and book stores—with care, of course.

Our interest, at least in this country, also undoubtedly comes from the *perceived* uniqueness of the event. It's perceived uniqueness was part of what shocked Americans in 1963, and probably still does today. Kennedy was actually the fourth president of the United States to be assassinated, but the preceding three assassinations had occurred between 1865 (President Lincoln) and 1901 (President McKinley)— a "long time ago," at least by American standards. While most of the world sees current events within the broader perspective of their county's many centuries of history, we in the United States tend to view events from within the more limited perspective of a total history of just over 200 years. To that extent, we are probably afflicted with our own unique brand of historical myopia. We may recognize that numerous assassinations of heads of state have occurred over the course of world history, but we tend to believe that the United States has been exempt from the turmoil and conflict that has characterized the politics of other countries—certainly, such things don't and shouldn't happen in twentieth century America, since "they never have before!" So when it happened in 1963, it shocked us, and it continues even today to challenge our notions about our country.

Will there ever be an end
to new conspiracy theories?

The Kennedy case is perhaps the world's greatest murder mystery. Like any good murder mystery, it has an abundance of fascinating evidence and misleading clues. But what makes the Kennedy case so much better than all of the rest?

Mystery novels, television shows, and movies have taught us that murders are solved by analyzing the evidence to determine who had the motive, opportunity and means to commit the crime. Murder mysteries typically hold our attention and challenge our minds by teasing us with "false clues" and dead-end theories—all pointing to different suspects who, in the end, when all becomes clear, are shown to be innocent when a Perry Mason-extracted confession or some other revelation exposes the true perpetrator.

Even in real trials, this motive-opportunity-means format is often used by the prosecution to prove its case, because it provides a way to logically organize and analyze all of the circumstantial evidence, evidence from which the guilt of the alleged perpetrator(s) of the murder can be inferred indirectly from all of the surrounding circumstances. This is a common format simply because direct evidence often is not available. The commission of a murder is typically not filmed, or tape recorded. Seldom do criminals write down their plan in advance, or leave behind a hand-written account to memorialize their success. Sometimes the weight of the circumstantial evidence finally becomes too great for the real culprit to bear and he confesses, making the jury's job (generally) fairly easy. Sometimes, the jury is asked to make a more difficult decision, whether the "circumstantial evidence" alone establishes guilt "beyond a reasonable doubt." Sometimes, things are even more complicated, and the jury is asked to decide which to believe, the prosecution's circumstantial case or a different circumstantial case proffered by the defense. Seldom is it more complicated than that.

The Kennedy case started as a typical murder case. Although many pictures were taken in Dealey Plaza at the time the shots were fired, both stills and movies, no film contained an image clear enough to identify the shooter, or shooters. There was no confession. The prime suspect, Lee Harvey Oswald was killed less than 48 hours after the murder, before giving any coherent or believable account of his actions. The other principal "suspect," Jack Ruby, killed Oswald while Oswald was in police custody—an event that raised a lot of new issues, and provided no real answers to anything—and then never gave any particularly credible explanation of his motivation for doing so. (Earl Ruby, in testimony before the Select Committee, said that his brother Jack told him that "when Oswald walked out of that doorway [into the police station parking garage] he had a silly smirk on his face as though it seemed to Jack he really felt good about it, and that is when Jack lost control of himself and shot him.")

Ruby never admitted having any prior association with Oswald, and like Oswald, he never admitted any involvement in the assassination of the president. Ruby asked Chief Justice Earl Warren several times during the Warren Commission's visit to the Dallas County Jail on June 7, 1964, to take him to Washington, stating that he had important things to reveal:

> RUBY: There is only one thing. If you don't take me back to Washington tonight to give me a chance to prove to the President that I am not guilty, then you will see the most tragic thing that will ever happen. And if you don't have the power to take me back, I won't be around to be able to prove my innocence or guilt. Now up to this moment, I have been talking with you for how long?
>
> Chief Justice WARREN: I would say for the better part of 3 hours.
>
> RUBY: All right, wouldn't it be ridiculous for me to speak sensibly all this time and give you this climactic talk that I have? Maybe something can be saved, something can

be done. What have you got to answer to that, Chief Justice Warren?

Chief Justice WARREN: Well, I don't know what can be done, Mr. Ruby, because I don't know what you anticipate we will encounter.

Representative GERALD FORD: Is there anything more you can tell us if you went back to Washington?

RUBY: Yes; are you sincere in wanting to take me back?

Representative FORD: We are most interested in all the information you have.

RUBY: All I know is maybe something can be saved. Because right now, I want to tell you this, I am used as a scapegoat, and there is no greater weapon that you can use to create some falsehood about some of the Jewish faith, especially at the terrible heinous crime such as the killing of President Kennedy. Now maybe something can be saved. It may not be too late, whatever happens, if our President, Lyndon Johnson, knew the truth from me. But if I am eliminated, there won't be any way of knowing. Right now, when I leave your presence now, I am the only one that can bring out the truth to our President, who believes in righteousness and justice.

The Warren Commission refused Ruby's request. Ruby died of cancer in January 1967 without ever revealing what he purportedly wanted to say. What was left was circumstantial evidence and the motive, opportunity and means analysis.

To that extent, the Kennedy case is a typical murder case, but that is where all similarities with "typical" murder cases end. It is the greatest murder case of all time not solely because of its fascinating evidence and theories; but because more investigation has always and probably will always produce more and more plausible conspiracy theories, and the circumstantial evidence and motive-opportunity-means analysis has been and always will be incapable of determining which theory is correct. The most fascinating mysteries are the unsolved mysteries.

In a typical murder case, the police and the prosecutor usually have limited resources, so when a solution appears that seems to fit the initial circumstantial evidence, they quit investigating. The "choices" given a jury are thus few. In the Kennedy case, the original Warren Commission investigation (even with its myopic focus) was extraordinarily extensive by usual standards. Subsequent private studies, coupled with the Select Committee's investigation, over the years have created an overall body of data that is now so massive and so intriguing and so provocative that the case seems to have acquired a life of its own—with the cycle of analysis, investigation and more analysis becoming perpetual. One great irony is that the Warren Commission might have been better able to convince the public that Oswald was a lone assassin if they had done *even less* investigation of the conspiracy issues, for the Warren Commission's own evidence (which they routinely rejected as lacking credibility) has provided much of the fuel for the criticisms of its conclusions and for further investigation.

The basic phenomenon is illustrated by the maxim of criminal defense lawyers who say, "If there is only one eyewitness to the crime my client is charged with, I've really got a problem. But if there are two, or better yet, three eye-witnesses who saw him do it, I've got a fighting chance of getting the jury to acquit him." The more evidence there is, the more ways there are to interpret it. To see what this means in the context of the Kennedy case, take the simple question of motive. Any analysis of the issue of motive must begin with the Kennedy presidency. Here is how that Presidency was described in the final Report of the Select Committee on Assassinations:

> In an era when the United States was confronted with intractable, often dangerous, international and domestic issues, the Kennedy administration was inevitably surrounded by controversy as it made policies to deal with the problems it faced. Although a popular President, John F. Kennedy was reviled by some, an enmity inextricably related to his policies. The possibility of nuclear holocaust overshadowed the administration's reshaping of cold war foreign policy as it grappled with Cuba, Berlin, Laos, Vietnam, relations in the Third World and Western Europe, and U.S. military strength. At home, an emerging Black protest movement, persistent unemployment, poverty and urban blight, governmental disorganization, congressional resistance to the President's New Frontier program, and the menace of organized crime were among the problems Kennedy faced.

But Kennedy did not merely face these problems. He took decisive, strong and often extremely unpopular actions to address the problems, and those actions severely threatened the powerful groups who held the vested interests that Kennedy was bent on destroying. The list of potential suspects who had the motive to eliminate "the Kennedy threat" is thus as long as the "membership lists" of all of the powerful groups who held the vested interests that his presidency threatened to destroy.

How many suspects are there who had the motive, opportunity, and means to kill Kennedy? The answer lies in the answer to other questions. How many covert operatives were there in this country who were working directly or indirectly for Castro? How many Mafia members were there in 1963? How many southern right wing extremists wanted to stop Kennedy's liberal civil rights movement? How many Black militants were dissatisfied with the progress that Kennedy was making—the progress that (from their perspective) he had promised and failed to deliver? How many CIA agents, and how many anti-Castro Cuban operatives with whom the CIA worked throughout the South, were furious over what they believed to be Kennedy's breech of faith, if not actual disloyalty to the United States, in withholding the air cover and abandoning them to be killed and captured on the beaches of Cuba during the Bay of Pigs invasion in 1961. How many CIA agents and anti-Castro Cuban operatives were furious with Kennedy for abandoning his promise to recover the Cuban homeland from Castro by making a non-invasion pledge with Russia in order to settle the Cuban missile crisis in 1962? In short, the list of suspects with a motive may not be infinite, but the mere creation of the list of names is certainly a worthy project for supercomputer Deep Blue.

Nor does the addition of the concept of "opportunity"

in the motive/opportunity/means trilogy significantly shorten the list of suspects. Kennedy was frequently accessible and often vulnerable to assassination in the manner that it finally actually occurred. In fact, there was more than one documented conversation prior to the assassination where the possibility of shooting him with a rifle from a building during a motorcade was discussed. The fact that such conversations occurred has led to other speculation, and more detailed investigation of the events surrounding the planning of the motorcade. Greater investigation in some cases has allowed earlier theories to be dismissed, such as the theory that the decision not to use the "protective bubble" over his convertible limousine during the Dallas motorcade on November 22, 1963 was part of a conspiracy. That theory seems to have been incorrect since the evidence indicates that Kennedy himself made the decision not to use the protective bubble, and further because the bubble was not bullet proof in any case, and only provided "protection" from the rain. Other theories have persisted.

The "opportunity" component of the motive, opportunity and means analysis is really of little assistance whenever a public figure is assassinated, at least in a free country such as the United States, since there have traditionally been severe limitations upon the ability of the Secret Service to keep the president alive if someone really wants to shoot him. The problem recalls to mind the alleged saying of a Mafia boss, that "If history has proven anything, it is that anyone can be killed."

But, you may ask, doesn't the list of suspects get much shorter on a practical basis when you ask which of those groups with motive, also had the *means* to kill Kennedy. Not particularly. The Russians, Fidel Castro (who our CIA had plotted to assassinate, and who knew of the plots), the pro-Castro Cubans, the anti-Castro Cubans (who had numerous para-military camps strewn from Florida through Louisiana, and were armed and in training for their own anticipated re-invasions of Cuba in 1963), our own military, our own CIA, the Black militants, the right wing extremists, and the Mafia, all had the means to kill Kennedy. They were, as the saying goes, certainly all "armed and dangerous."

Aren't Oswald's Associates
the Only Real Conspiracy Suspects?

No, for several reasons. It is true that the evidence tends to strongly indicate that Oswald was a shooter in Dealey Plaza and shot at least some—probably all—of the bullets that found their way into the presidential limousine. Thus, it might at first appear possible to weed out the list of suspects using the motive, opportunity and means analysis, and limit the list to Oswald's associates, upon the rationale that it is not merely a question of having *any* means available to kill the president, but having access to *the means* that was actually used, namely, Oswald.

Of course, this is a logical, and perhaps first place to

start, and as I noted earlier, the Select Committee used this rationale and tried to investigate at least those of Oswald's "associates" who we were able to identify. Even that first step is a daunting task, since Oswald led a circuitous, and perplexing life. He had renounced his citizenship and lived in Russia, and his activities were clearly monitored by the Russian KGB. Hence, by this limited analysis, Russia had access to *the means* to kill the president, since Oswald had extensive contacts with Russia. In the summer of 1963, Oswald was running around in New Orleans with David Ferrie. Ferrie was a militant anti-Castro operative, and associated both with the right-wing activities at 544 Camp Street and the anti-Castro military training camps in the New Orleans area, hence the right-wing extremists and anti-Castro Cubans had direct access to "the means."

Ferrie was also an investigator for Carlos Marcello, the head of the Mafia in Louisiana, and during the summer of 1963, Oswald was living in New Orleans with his Uncle, Charles "Dutz" Murret, who worked in the Marcello gambling organization. So the Mafia clearly had access to "the means."

Oswald's other activities and the suspicious events strewn throughout his perplexing life, including his earlier having been a U.S. Marine and then later having traveled to and from Russia with too much "apparent ease," led people to suspect that he was perhaps a CIA operative (i.e., never really a Russian defector, but a U.S. agent sent to Russia). Without even evaluating the strength of such evidence, it certainly can hardly be denied that the CIA could have had contacts with Oswald at almost any point they desired, and the evidence is clear that the CIA at least at some points in time did have contact with many of Oswald's associates.

In the summer of 1963, Oswald was in contact with the Fair Play for Cuba group and handed out pro-Castro fliers in New Orleans. Shortly before the assassination, Oswald visited the Cuban consulate in Mexico City. Thus, the Cuban conspiracy theories had a factual basis at least to the extent of demonstrable access to "the means."

The great murder mystery is even greater, however, because the scope of the problem is even bigger: any investigative approach must necessarily also consider the possibility of *indirect* access to Oswald. If, for example, the Mafia wanted to kill Kennedy, is it reasonable to assume that a Mafia boss would have contacted Oswald directly? No. To take another example, if the government (e.g., the CIA) had been involved, would a CIA agent, employed directly by the agency, have met with Oswald? Not likely. They would have used what in intelligence community circles is often referred to as a "cut-out." At least to the extent that any conspiracy may have involved a professional organization, particularly one having clandestine operational capabilities (Russian KGB, Cuban DGI, Mafia, CIA, military intelligence, etc.), the "investigative hypotheses" must necessarily include the possible use of an intermediary who could be trusted to never talk, and/or who could be "disposed of" afterwards, if necessary. (This possibility, of course, is the reason that all of "the mysterious deaths" have been so interesting.) So, any rational analysis of the number of suspects, or groups of suspects, must include at a minimum all of the *associates of the associates* of Oswald.

In short, the Kennedy case is perhaps the greatest murder mysteries of all time because of the extraordinary magnitude of evidence and plausible possible solutions—"a solution for everyone"—and the inability to narrow the possible theories down to probabilities upon the basis of a motive, opportunity and means analysis. In fact, the principal result of continued investigation and the search for better and more definitive evidence has been the expansion of possible solutions, not the elimination of them. This may be the final irony of the Kennedy case, the explanation for its continued life, and the reason that interest in it will never die. In most murder cases, more evidence is a *help* in solving the case, since it tends to eliminate possible suspects, and produce probable answers about the identity of the true perpetrator. In the Kennedy case, as more evidence is gathered, more theories will always be forthcoming, because the number of suspects that had the motive, the opportunity, and the means to kill the president—even if not actually infinite—is certainly interminable.

*Will direct evidence ever be uncovered
revealing the true facts?*

The short answer is that I saw the difficulty in secur-
ing such evidence when we conducted the investigation in
1977–78. That was fifteen years after the fact. Now it is
thirty-five years after the fact. Even if we assume that someone in a position to confess (a conspirator) is still alive, and
might still come forward, the credibility of a confession
would be difficult to evaluate.

I do believe that more definitive answers could be secured about the number and origins of shots that were fired
if the additional testing recommended by Bolt, Beranek and
Newman were effectively and impartially pursued. But there
is little, if any, remaining physical evidence from the original
crime scene from which, even with more analysis, an additional conspirator is likely to be identified. Even if "new"

physical evidence were "discovered," authenticating it might present insurmountable problems at this late date. The inherent difficulty surrounding such matters as the "chain of custody" of physical evidence was illustrated in the O.J. Simpson trial, where the elapsed time was only hours or days, instead of decades.

Even in 1978, ascertaining the credibility of witness testimony after fifteen years was tough. As the years go on, the problem of judging credibility—which merely *starts* with basic problems of recollection—becomes geometrically magnified by the increasing difficulty in assessing the impact of the complex of human interests, biases, and motives that twist and shape and often cause wholesale fabrication of testimony. Getting significantly more definitive answers than we already have, for these reasons, seems unlikely.

But nothing is inevitable. A new photo, a new motion picture record, a new scientific technique for extracting even greater detail from old fuzzy films or even better data from old scratchy tape recordings, or perhaps even the ultimate disclosure of some long-classified document, may still open a door to "the ultimate answer." After all, through determination and that proverbial hope-that-springs-eternal, the secrets of treasure ships buried for hundreds of years have been reclaimed from their watery graves, so. . .

To Order Additional Copies

For credit card orders, call Toll Free: 1-877-535-1998

Or, submit your credit card order via the Internet:
http://www.jfkassassination.com

Or, mail check or money order to:
   Paleface Press
   P.O. Box 696
   Spicewood, Texas 78669
Please include with your order your:

Name	
Street Address	
City	
State	
Zip Code	
Telephone #	
# of books ordered	

Price: $24.95, plus $4.95 for shipping and handling. (Only a single fee of $4.95 for shipping and handling is charged per order, for any order of 1 to 5 books.)

Please call for wholesale pricing
on orders of more than 5 books.